THE NIGHT GARDENER

THE NIGHT GARDENER

MARJORIE SANDOR

THE LYONS PRESS

Printed in the United States of America
10 9 8 7 6 5 4 3 2 1

Library of Congress Cataloging-in-Publication Data
Sandor, Marjorie.
    The night gardener / Marjorie Sandor.
        p.   cm.
    ISBN 1-55821-931-5
        1. Sandor, Marjorie. 2. Women authors, American—20th century—
Biography.   I. Title
    PS3569.A5195Z47   1999
    813'.54—dc21
    [B]   99-22601
                                                      CIP

Some of the essays in *The Night Gardener* have previously appeared in *The Georgia
Review*, *House Beautiful*, *The Gift of Trout*, *The Most Wonderful Book*, *The New York Times*,
The New York Times Magazine, and *Victoria*.

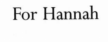

For Hannah

CONTENTS

1

2

3

4

PART

1

YOU WITH YOUR NOSE
IN A BOOK

I don't remember reading my first book so much as smelling
it. This was a folktale collection called *Tales Told Under the
Green Umbrella*, and by the time it got to me—I was the
youngest of four—its green covers were spotted with pungent
mold and the spine was rubbed bald at the tips, all the little
threads exposed. The pages, like those of my father's ancient
army pocketbooks of Steinbeck and O'Hara, were a pale
brown with yellowed edges. But my book had a different bouquet, dry and infinitely more delicate—you had to put your
nose into it to get the full effect.

Of all its pages, the *Umbrella*'s most pleasurable was the
dangerously thin sheet of tissue paper over the frontispiece,
which I riffled lightly, ceremonially, between my fingertips
before each reading. Once I was inside the stories, the pleasures
grew deeper hued, glossy, indestructible: pen-and-ink drawings
every four pages, and every fifteen, a shiny page illustrating a

dramatic moment in colors to long for afterward, and never find again. The palace garden was a dusky duck-egg green, the Chinese emperor's robe a dark sealing-wax red. Best of all was the hot gold-yellow of the magical apples rolling away from the princess on the glass hill, whose hair was just as bright.

A few years ago I rescued this book from my oldest brother's shelf: his children are long since grown, and my daughter, at the time, was five—exactly the age I was when my father first began reading it to me. The first story, in the manner of an overture, introduces Old Lukoie the Sandman, who blows sleep dust into little children's eyes as they sit before the fire on their quaint three-legged stools. If the children have been naughty, he holds over their heads a plain umbrella, and no dreams visit them that night. But if they've been good, he brings out his green umbrella, which turns and turns all night, bringing scene after vivid scene their way.

It strikes me that the books I love best now have precisely the kaleidoscopic effect of the green umbrella: that of constantly changing saturated colors and dramatic scenes. I am afraid of nothing more than the possibility of having the plain umbrella held dully over my head, and still long for the unexpected turns of old folktales, for imprisonments and escapes, foolish mistakes and last-minute changes of heart. I confess to a particular weakness for tales of unrequited love and interminable delays, and love best those writers whose voices sing like the old storytellers and who walk a tightrope between the real world and the fantastic one of dreams: E. T. A. Hoffmann,

Franz Kafka, William Faulkner, Christina Stead, Gabriel García Márquez. Best of all is Eudora Welty, who holds time still in ordinary towns and ordinary lives by shading them with pagan and biblical mythologies—stories read aloud to her by her mother in deepest childhood. In these writers there is a touch of the vaudeville and the circus, an imaginative abundance that never wears you out, because beneath it lies a perfect pitch for detail and drama, until finally a truth is briefly caught—gracefully, barely, exactly in the way of a circus performer in midair, catching the swinging trapeze.

The smell of that first book is mixed up for me now with the smell of my father, long since passed away, so there is also something of yearning and loss mixed up in my love of reading. I remember the smell of him as he read: a peppery odor that came off his black hair and his red cardigan, even his leather chair. With that smell came the voice I'm always looking for in books: the melodic leftovers of Yiddish with a velvety rumbling underneath, like that of some sleeping volcano, a rough music to lull and worry the listener all at once. It was always after dinner that he read to me, and his big stomach sang harmony while he read. I listened to that, too, from my place smashed close up against his side in the leather chair, my arm going numb in the brief paradise of his attention before he yawned hugely and sent me to bed.

My father, like all fathers, had his favorite tale. This was the *Three Billy Goats Gruff*, which displayed most beautifully his fearsome and gravelly bass, his pleasure in exaggerating the musical scale and volume of everyday speech. I knew he was tired when he called me to the chair for my nightly story; that soon enough, he would be closing the book and giving me a little push, "to bed now, before Old Lukoie the Sandman gets you," the little aggravations of grown-up life creeping back into his voice, turning it ordinary again. But he always saved his strength, his biggest effort, for the last and biggest Billy Goat Gruff. "Who's that walking on my bridge?" he'd rumble. "It is I, the Third Billy Goat Gruff." I trembled, the other arm going stiff, knowing the finale was close. We'd be nearly there, right at the penultimate moment, reaching for the crisis, when my mother would appear in the doorway, waving her dish towel at him.

"You're scaring her," she'd say.

And he: "Poo—she loves it!"

They were both right, of course, my mother and my father, those two people forever in disagreement, between whom there must have hovered some faint truth, some right answer. Maybe that's the moment that made me grow up loving literature, sniffing and feasting and terrified all at once, suspended in that moment just before the story ends and I am sent to bed to dream my own.

THE GOLDEN AGE

Every family has its lost paradise, if you go back far enough. Ours was a little house in Alhambra, a town in the San Gabriel valley northeast of Los Angeles. I never actually came to know the house for myself—we moved from it a few months after I was born—but even the name Alhambra is enough to drive me mad with desire and regret, and not exactly for sunlight and Spanish fountains. Old family pictures, as well as place-names, are designed to hurt you for life. In ours, the small quaint bungalow shimmers in a veritable Eden: there are terraces of fragrant orange trees, of fig and olive and plum, and the fabled redwood that the youngest of my three big brothers spent most of his time in—from the loss of which, my mother says, he has never quite recovered. When she says this, she looks at me meaningfully, as if I got born on purpose, to break the spell of those years.

But how can this be, when I'm under the spell too, under

the spell of photographs that haunt by their edges and omissions, by what must surely lie just beyond the frame? The terraces themselves were said to slope by degrees down to a tiled swimming pool and a tennis court, the site of my parents' summer extravaganzas. *Nightclub Under the Stars* these parties were called, fund-raisers for their new synagogue. It is hard to connect these occasions to religion: in family pictures, they look like wild, deliciously primitive cocktail-bacchanals. My mother is a svelte Cleopatra in white with gold rickrack, my father an awkward Marc Antony, his wig slightly askew. There are lovers in hedges, cars driven up on neighbors' lawns, and in the morning, fake Spanish doubloons and real dimes for my brothers to find in the cracks of the tennis court, jiggled out of mens' trousers while a dance band played and couples engaged in the cha-cha, the Charleston, and, at midnight, less imaginable embraces.

The small size of the house is no disappointment to me. It is, in fact, the most mysterious part of my homesickness: for years I was convinced that there had once been a great mansion on the property, now vanished, and that we had lived in the servants' quarters or the "carriage house," a phrase I must have picked up from a book and liked the sound of. I liked even better the idea that we were living ignorantly on the grounds of a former estate, feasting off an old orchard's fruit, after a revolution or some other disaster that had conveniently removed the previous, wealthy inhabitants, who hovered ghostlike now, especially during my parents' costume parties.

Doubtless I got all this from F. Scott Fitzgerald in moony adolescence, but it was, in some measure, encouraged by the strange habits of my family—and maybe destiny itself. Nobody ever took me back to Almansor Street to set me straight, though we had moved only one town away. Did I never ask to go there, or did they put me off, gently, carefully, not wanting to remind me of my inadvertent crime in having been born— the last and accidental child, the one who made the house too small?

So it was that my course was set. From day one, orphan of the golden age, I lived on family photos, hungrily, the way none of my brothers would, with longing and misplaced passion for these pictures, which have themselves been corrupted by time. I love particularly the way time has darkened the dark red of my mother's lipstick, turned the white frame mustard yellow, washed a fainter yellow over the skin of my two oldest brothers, sitting close together and holding the black cocker spaniel who died famously of a heart attack during a lightning storm—before I was born, of course. And the most faded photograph of all, dimmer every year, is one of the youngest of my brothers, in his beloved redwood tree. It's so shadowy you can barely tell his limbs apart from the tree's, and he gazes out, a pair of eyes and a shock of bright hair, sullen and beautiful, as if he has just been told to come down, forever.

If this wasn't enough, the very way our family keeps snapshots is an invitation to yearn, to distort, to reinvent if necessary, for the pictures are not properly set in albums with dates and little captions to guide you through the years, but kept in old leather boxes in a basement cupboard. There might be a date and a name on the back of one, but there might not be, either. The truth is probably quite simple. My parents were too busy to catalog their lives: too busy with the four of us, my father's medical practice, the social life of the synagogue, our family's steady rise into the upper-middle class. The very disorder of the photographs seems to suggest that they had no time to look back, nor any reason to as the gathering wave of their assimilation carried them up and up; soon there are no more images of the fruit trees, of tipsy bewigged adults raising their glasses to the camera, of my brothers in a blur of play with the Rodriguez children from a few blocks over. Soon there are pictures of the new house in the wealthy suburb of San Marino two miles north: a bigger house, a semicircular driveway, a Monterey pine out front, carefully trimmed in topiary shape. Nowhere in its branches could a child hide from view.

But these pictures belong to me now. I am the one, out of the four of us, who wants them most. I want them as much for what they don't tell as for what they do. They have given me, by beautiful accident, a way of reading family history that is liberated from chains of fact. A story—any story—can grow here, and meanwhile, there is always the tantalizing possibility that a picture unseen is yet left at the bottom of the box, or in another one somewhere else. Not thrown away, simply missing.

I tried once, in my early twenties, to rid myself of this nostalgia, this penchant for inaccuracy, to once and for all get practical and realistic, and maybe, too, get rid of the old childhood guilt that it was all my fault we'd moved. I got the Almansor Street address from my mother and drove past. I nearly held my breath as I drove closer—what ancient monument, blanketed in heavy green vines, did I imagine I would come upon?

But this is California, after all. The celebrated spot had long since vanished, leaving no trace. There, where it should have been, was a glittering white stucco building called Shangri-La Apartments. No fruit trees, no redwood, no terraces descended to anything, though there was a pool, fenced and surrounded by blinding white, a hot white echo of absence.

There was nothing to stop me from dreaming now. By disappearing before I could see it, the lost domain would be forever remembered. So am I doomed to eternal homesickness, witness to the maybe, and haunted by the certainty—not so terrible after all—that I missed the truth and my family's golden age all at once: a perception perhaps given divinely unto all last, late, and accidental children.

PIANO FOR FOUR HANDS

My mother, who is the musician in our family, waited years for a miracle: for one of us to fall in love with the piano. Her tactical shift was so quiet I never guessed what was afoot. "Just tell me when you're settled down, and I'll send the Yamaha," she said, long-distance, a little breathless, as if the migratory patterns of my generation left her slightly winded. This was the way her domestic magic worked: she waited until I married and set up housekeeping in a small Boston apartment, and let me discover for myself that something was wrong, missing from our living room.

"Of course," she said casually. "You need the piano."

How far back had she planted the seeds of my awakening? There was always a piano in our house when I was growing up, as much a feature in daily life as any bed or kitchen table. Our first was an upright, and even its placement in our chaotic "family room" seems to me now a sign of her foresight.

For while we were using the piano as an obstacle in our games of tag, and its bench as a place to hide things, it was being secretly rooted in our memories, in our vision of what belongs in a home.

My mother herself is an organist, and all the years of our childhood she kept her Hammond organ safely out of the way of domestic traffic, in our best room, our forbidden room. This was her private domain. Entering it, you crossed the border between earthly distraction and divine art; the noises of kitchen and family room were distant and muffled against the ever-complicating Toccata and Fugue in D Minor. Evenings, she dabbled in the sublime: Bach, Franck, and Duruflé. Then, like a good wife of her generation, she came down to earth and played tunes from *South Pacific* to keep my father happy.

Once in a while she let me sit on the bench with her and improvise dramatic scenes: "Storm at Sea," I remember, and "Graveyard at Midnight," in which I tolled heavy low notes on full vibrato, bringing myself to rapturous tears of invented grief. But mostly I lay on the fancy pale gold carpet of that room, watching her feet cross and speed over the pedals: the deep trembling notes of the organ accompanied by the music of evening insects, the darkening shapes of the live oaks and palms of our backyard.

Each of us began piano lessons promptly at the age of seven; none of us blossomed. At fourteen, one of my brothers switched to guitar and got as far as "Norwegian Woods"; another one switched too, and memorized the opening bars of "Classical Gas." I was next. After a year of lessons, I suffered through a monumental one-page minuet, then strode to my mother.

"Listen! I can play it good," I said.

"Well," she said quietly. "You can play it well."

That night, with the pencil kept at the piano for lesson time, I carved, in small, distinct letters, the word *Well* into the soft wood of the lid.

I was sent to my room, but for years after, I noted the little blemish with triumph and amazement at my own nerve, pressing my fingers over the grooves of my careful childhood script as if it were a battle scar, my first serious mark on the world.

The upright was eventually delivered to my oldest brother's house, where their first child would be born—my mother was thinking ahead, as usual. Back at our house, perhaps figuring me safely past the age of impromptu wood carving, she ordered the Yamaha, an ebony baby grand, and when it arrived she directed the movers to put it deep in the belly of our house, in the carpeted basement room where we kept photo albums and relics of family outings. She did not suggest lessons; she simply shrugged and gave me the same resigned smile she'd fixed on the movers. I was slightly hurt that she did not insist on lessons, that she would hide such a beautiful and costly instrument in an out-of-the-way spot, where guests would not be able to hear it. But such is the nature of maternal wisdom:

eerily accurate, reaching into the future with a lazy incandescence that dazzles you only after it's too late. While I subjected the Yamaha to the same three or four chords every day in variations of current folk-rock, my mother waited patiently. Sometimes she sat behind me, quietly tapping out the tempo on her knee. "You have a good ear," she'd say. "Someday you'll see you don't have to bang so hard."

In Boston, the piano fit with uncanny ease into our living room's bay window. It shone. It appeared to be waiting for something. I tried out a mournful Jackson Browne tune from the early seventies, and was mortified by the monotony of the progressions that had gripped me as an adolescent. I was acutely aware that at any minute my mother might call. Out of this mixture of minor embarrassment and guilt, I contacted a local music school and said, shakily, "Beginning intermediate."

My teacher was a dark-haired, severe Russian named Ludmilla who prescribed violent medicine: Czerny's School of Velocity. The first exercise in the book had no flats or sharps but was daunting nonetheless, with its command: *presto*, and its strenuous arpeggios and cadenzas. It was penance for a lifetime of musical and filial neglect, and I took it up with a sinner's compulsive certainty.

My mother was pleased, in a careful, reserved sort of way. "You're actually reading music," she said, as if this were one of the miracles in the desert—like manna or the burning bush. There was a little catch in her voice that surprised me.

"What are you working on these days?" I asked.

"Oh," she said lightly. "My fingers are a little stiff. I stopped a while ago."

I was too stunned to answer, and in her unfailing sense of domestic grace, she quickly added that she was of course keeping the organ for her grandchildren. "They love to bang on it so," she said.

A single, indecent year after she sent the piano east, we moved, this time to the South and university teaching jobs. I was very nearly afraid to tell her, as if, after claiming to settle down, I'd broken some unspoken pact.

Where would the piano go in our new house, our first?

It was destined, of course, to fit only in one place, a low-ceilinged "rumpus room" in the far back of the house, a room we'd already lined with books and family pictures. This was not the best place for a piano, with its big picture windows on two sides and a steamy private jungle of vines and sable palm all around. But it felt protected back there, comfortable; it was where, as a family, we spent our evening time.

After a year of Florida humidity, little milky spots appeared on the Yamaha's beautiful black sides. Tuners began to visit our house, shaking their heads over the terminal patient, prescribing not one but two little black heating tubes to regulate its internal weather.

Still, it felt good to be playing again, to start lessons with a new instructor, especially one who favored Mozart over

Czerny, even for finger exercises. But our third spring in Florida I found I was so sleepy I couldn't stay awake long enough in the evening to practice. Pure laziness, I thought, or too much schoolwork, but my mother, long-distance, knew better. Over the nine months we waited for our baby's arrival, whole evenings passed in which it seemed enough to simply *look* at the piano from the depths of the rumpus room couch.

Soon enough the great instrument was reduced to a dark spot behind my left shoulder—the one with the little white towel draped across it—and our newborn daughter herself, head bobbing, was nodding as if in secret communication with it. Months went by: no Mozart, not even Jackson Browne. The Yamaha itself was now cluttered with little soft pale toys, pale laundry in heaps.

My mother, who had come to see the baby, sighed when she saw where we had put the piano. "I guess there really isn't anywhere else," she said. It was a day or two before she tactfully, almost shyly, mentioned the dust on the lid. "You should play," she said. "I always played when they slept."

It would be over a year before I managed to make good on this suggestion. But miraculously, one afternoon while Hannah slept, I found myself at the piano with a book of Mozart sonatas, its pages gummed together from the humidity. Just beyond the big windows, in the sable palm, in the oaks of our yard, the cicadas made a fierce, metallic racket, and suddenly it sounded like home, like those early-evening hours in my childhood, when I lay on my belly watching my mother play.

Hunched over the keys, hair in my face, with the slumped posture of my teenaged self, I noticed that I was reading. Breathing, thinking. Start pianissimo, begin the crescendo here. A phrase emerged in a minor key, resolved, and came back major—Mozart's passion for comedy in the midst of the sublimely sad. Here were the forms, earthly and celestial, my mother had loved all her life, and once made with her fingers. I wanted to call her and say, "Mother, listen," but I made a little deal with myself: get through the Rondo first.

That's where I was, laboring along at half speed, when I heard Hannah waking up from her nap. A minute later she appeared at the door of the rumpus room and scrambled up onto the piano bench with a single hoist, her feet flipping up behind her in the air like a seal flinging itself onto a warm rock.

She pushed my hands off the keys.

"Hannah play," she said.

What she wanted to play, it turned out, was the bass, the low, tolling bells and gloom of my old "Graveyard at Midnight." I pressed my foot to the sustain pedal as she situated herself. And with a straight back and fat, greedy, beautiful hands, she banged away at the deepest notes in the world.

BROOKIES AND BABIES

The summer after our daughter was born, my husband discovered a passion for nature photography. We'd rented a cabin in central Colorado for our summer vacation, and he'd bought a new camera, a tripod too. He rose at dawn and departed again just before sunset. "The light is perfect—I've got to go," he'd whisper cautiously, but it didn't matter—uncannily, the baby woke up just as the door closed behind him.

Nursing her in the chill morning air, something came back to me: my own father's obsession with photography, then rare books, then coins. Groggily, I theorized that the Family Man's habit of acquiring expensive equipment was a brilliant tactic for sudden escape—one that a first-time mother with a touch of cabin fever might do well to imitate. I also noted that I could never voluntarily rise at dawn: whatever I did would have to be slow, lazy, and situated at a time of day when pioneer gumption wasn't required.

My husband's boyhood spinning rod and tackle box leaned against the wall of the cabin's mud porch, and it occurred to me that the forty-dollar cost of a nonresident fishing license was a modest but clear reply to the camera and tripod. As I plotted the hours I would steal, my arms and breasts tingled— just as they did when Hannah cried out in the night. Motherhood was making me conscious, for the first time, of the symbiotic tangle of our lives, of the body's precise sense of justice when it comes to babies, food, and sleep. "Remember, you're still eating for two," the pediatrician had said, but this hadn't prepared me for those depth-charge hungers, or the silky fog I slipped under at ten in the morning—not the desire for sleep, but the sleep itself, now, and not later.

But watching Bob return from his early-morning trips, his expression suggesting that nothing less than a spiritual transformation had taken place, I dimly imagined what it might feel like to be alone, really alone, for a whole afternoon; how a solitary drive up the road into the mysterious lap of the mountains to our east might turn up a series of small but satisfying revelations, one after another.

A harmless little plan, but as I made it, there was Hannah, trying to sit up on the bed, helplessly curved over her tiny square Picasso feet. I had the uneasy feeling that I myself had put her in this pose. When I lifted her into my arms, she looked me dead in the eye and buzzed her lips like a big kid. The tingling rushed through me again. There was no telling what miracles I was going to miss.

∽

Not knowing where to begin, I went to our postmaster, known to locals as "R.D." He'd welcomed us warmly when we arrived, and weighed Hannah on the postal scale. He was about fifty, with one eye always looking off to the side as if he had two visions: one for the post office and one for some secret, otherworldly vocation.

It turned out to be so. By the speed at which he hauled out his map, it seemed he'd been waiting for this. He telephoned friends up a local stream and got me permission to fish the creek that ran through their property. With his rubber postmaster's thimble holding down the map, he pointed out his own favorite rivers and dreamily chanted the names of those further away: the Fryingpan, the Curecanti, Crystal Creek.

I told him I couldn't go that far, and he cocked his head patiently. Was he waiting for me to explain that sure, the baby could take a bottle from Bob, but I had to get home in time for the next feeding or risk a fiery heat in my breasts, leaking milk, and, as the pediatrician sternly put it, "a falloff in production"?

R.D.'s friends lived about a forty-minute drive up a curvy gravel road clogged with grazing cattle dutifully nursing their young. I unchained three cattle gates and carefully—why was I shaking?—chained them up again. At the house, a handsome matriarch named Betty Hawk pointed me toward a dense line of cottonwoods; our conversation was convivial but brief, as if she, like R.D., knew exactly how much to give the passing pilgrim.

Almost immediately I lost myself in the brush and caught my rod in the trees. Glancing at my watch, I saw that I'd missed Hannah's afternoon feeding. By way of reply, my breasts stung and swelled up tight, and I had a sudden vision of a turkey sandwich. A huge buck vaulted past, and a few minutes later, a dusty, tea-colored snake hooked its way across a clearing. These seemed like omens, though of what I could not say.

What I remember of that first day: finding the creek and casting into a deep pool, and how, just as the water darkened under a late-afternoon cloud, I felt a small shock travel up my palm, a tug like a code from the invisible world. I was instantly reminded of Hannah, and the little surge of adrenaline I always got as she shook her head, wild with hunger, her mouth opening for the latch-on. "Take it," I wanted to say to the fish, feeling that sudden power. "Come on, baby, this is it."

A month later, Hannah began to sit up on her own. Soon after, she learned to ring the miniature dinner bell on the cabin wall, and Bob moved it down low so she could ring it anytime she pleased. She laughed her first real laugh, and buzzed her lips for our landlord. Three afternoons a week, Bob held her up to the front windows as I turned the car toward the east; once, I was so sleepy I drove all the way to Betty Hawk's place without my rod.

But I kept going back. I got tough with my worms, working them onto the hook with maternal exasperation. I snagged and unsnagged my line, ventured upstream and down, and learned to cast just so, into the riffles, the margins, the little pools. I caught trout: rainbows with their pink-sided glory, and slim, speckled native brook trout, or brookies—the only fish I know of that has a tender nickname, something you might call your baby.

One afternoon in late August, I came home with my best fish—a fine, fat brown trout. On the porch I stopped and knocked on the window, holding up my dripping catch for my family to admire. Hannah was sitting upright on the floor, ringing the little dinner bell. She looked different somehow: slimmer, smarter. I suddenly noticed she had more hair. Bob looked different too: harassed, patient, deeply amazed.

As I stood there with the fish, Hannah glanced up briefly, smiled, then bent again to her bell, and I felt the first little barb of the future, her discovery of solitary pleasures, apart from us.

A RIVER OF ONE'S OWN

I t seemed such a simple act, to take up fishing. I had a baby
daughter, the summer off from teaching, and a faint childhood memory of dangling a hook baited with Velveeta over
a small creek. I had no ambition; just wanted a cure for cabin
fever. But I am also the younger sister of three men, and in the
foolhardy way of little sisters, I telephoned one of them after
my first triumphant landing of a trout.

"Caught a brown tonight, thirteen inches."

"Nice," he said. "What'd you take it on?"

"A worm."

"Gross!" he cried. "You're kidding."

This particular brother was forty-five, a doctor, a Yale
graduate, and in his house a whole bookshelf was devoted to
the sacred texts of fly fishing. His lapse in diction revealed the
depth of my transgression. I might have broken one of the Ten
Commandments: Thou shalt not fish with worms.

I should have known better. When I was young, all three brothers were versed in the sacred rites of fly fishing. The length of time it took them to prepare for trips testified to its high mystery. Out of closets came hip waders, nets, special vests with a fuzzy strip for the flies. The names of the flies themselves—Humpy, Irresistible, Bitch Creek Special— called up the veiled hostility of the clubhouse password, the secret handshake, the posted sign: GIRLS KEEP OUT.

I kept my distance: their preparations carried a taboo as searing as my father's garage workbench, the school shop, and math, which I was failing. Yet as they departed, I trailed my brothers to our Pontiac and grasped the hot chrome of the door handle till my mother had to pry my fingers loose.

Eventually this dark era of exclusion passed. It was replaced by something far more formidable: nostalgia. My brothers settled in cities, and the great trout streams became places perpetually dappled and windless, brightened by the curving back of the Really Big One; places that now took suspiciously complex arrangements to get to. Whenever I suggested such a trip, my brothers simply sighed for their lost paradise.

Then, this summer, from our rented cabin near some of the greatest trout streams in the world, I called my middle brother.

Was it revenge or the old desire to get inside the clubhouse that made me tempt him back over the Garden wall? Over the telephone, I recited the names of the blue-ribbon streams in our vicinity, and listened patiently as he chanted, in his turn, the names of his favorite flies: Elk-Hair Caddis, the Royal Stimulator, and that worrisome Bitch Creek Special.

In the afternoons before venturing up to a nearby creek with my carton of worms, I put maps in the mail, marking the Taylor, the Fryingpan, and just twelve miles away, the mighty Gunnison.

I avoided thinking about my worms versus his flies. I took up my spinning rod and drove to my creek, secretly relishing the primitive indelicacies of worm fishing: the grit, the ooze, the real blood on my fingers as the little guys tried to squirm away from me and failed.

My brother arrived in July, pale, a little nervous, armed with his own maps. But the next morning he stood fully outfitted in khaki, waiting in our kitchen while I finished my breakfast. I saw with no small misgiving that he had brought an extra fly rod for me, and an ancient pair of waders, size eleven, mens. Our gear and lunches were already packed into a Boy Scout knapsack that bore two of my brothers' names and our child-hood address in heavy black marker.

An hour later, I was stumbling in the great boots and look-ing dizzily into the wide, fast waters of the Gunnison, a river that in no way resembled my little creek, with its mysterious pools and its message that trout, like paradise, exist only in the shadows where you can't see them.

My brother looked a little like a priest in his splendid re-galia, right down to the new hat and a graphite rod whose cost he would not reveal. Midstream, he fastened a wet fly to my leader (I was too stunned to ask its name), showed me a "simple cast," and moved away to cast a dry fly toward the bank. His arm eased back and forth, once, twice, as if invoking a spell, and the line arced and uncurled across the water. Where the fly touched down there was a flash, a sudden swirl.

"Yes," said my brother.

My own lowly rank was confirmed by his explanation (after playing a twenty-inch brown and slipping it gracefully into the net) that dry-fly fishing was a great deal more complicated than wet-fly fishing. The abyss opened before me: fly fishing now turned out to be divided into lower and higher arts. As I whipped my line over my head three times and watched it spiral into a small, failed coil on the water, he said consolingly, "It's an aesthetic thing, really. You're a part of the river; much more intimate than fishing with worms."

He handed me the net and creel. "Watch this," he said.

While I pondered my new status as an initiate, my brother got down to business. He caught his two- and three-pound rainbows, admired them, and released them into the stream. I seethed with the dark and ancient rage of younger sisters as I fell neatly into the role of acolyte. I held the net as he brought in an enormous curving rainbow, my legs far apart and the net gripped in both hands as if I were preparing to capture the river itself.

"Let's keep this one," I said.

He looked slightly aggrieved. I had violated yet another commandment: Thou shalt not kill trout. But after a decent interval, he acquiesced.

My brother's last fish was another rainbow, bigger than the last, and before he released it he held it above the river, his legs apart and his hat a little askew, as if posing for a souvenir photograph. This ceremonial display of the trophy finished me off: I'd been duped from the beginning, destined only to be witness for this lonely male triumph.

I handed him the creel. "You carry it back," I said. I might have been handing over my whole childhood worship and fear of missing out.

After my brother was safely out of the state, I went back to my creek. Crouched on the river stones, I chose a fat night crawler and slipped its shoulder onto the hook and up the shank. A few minutes later, I landed a rainbow, fifteen inches and barely hooked.

I held it sideways and admired it on both sides, waiting for aesthetic bliss and the feeling of oneness with the fish. I knew what should follow: the careful unhooking, the letting go. But I didn't, I couldn't. Worm fishers, like the unconverted, are a stubborn lot. I crouched on the bank to thwack the fish and gut it. The earthy smell of worm was on my hands and in my hair: this was private, messy, sinful. Intimate, I said to myself, not yearning after some dream of the ultimate this or that. But why was I theorizing if fishing with worms was such a humble act? Don't apologize, I commanded myself. Bring home the beautiful fish, fry it up, and place it before your family. "Eat," I would tell my daughter, my firstborn. "Eat, and learn to fish."

PART

2

THE NOVITIATE'S TALE

At the south end of Darby, Montana, right before the speed limit goes up and the Bitterroot River comes back into view, there's a Sinclair station with a marquee that looms like wish fulfillment. All in capital letters, like the message DRINK ME on the little bottle Alice finds, this marquee reads: DIESEL, UNLEADED, FLIES.

What is it about the prospect of trout fishing that turns the novitiate's simplest act—that of buying a couple of flies or a new leader—into a quest, a rite of passage? There was a long riffle just upstream from Darby that looked magical to me— it had to be full of rainbows—and waiting for the time to get there, I hungered for it as unrequitedly as I do for certain film stars and countries I'll never get to: secretly, with idiotic surges of adolescent chills and fever.

Practically speaking, I needed a leader. I strode to the screen door of the Sinclair station, heavily booted like any hero, but faintly aware of my relatively small size and deep ignorance. The whole business seemed a dazzling path to certain failure: wrong fly, too hot a day, too cold, wrong spot, wrong way to fish the right spot—infinite and thrilling were the ways.

In a small room beyond Wheat Thins and Jim's World-Famous Jerky, a man waited behind a glass case of flies, reading the newspaper with the tricky nonchalance of all guardians of the dreamworld. A few packets of hooks and spools of fishing line hung on a pegboard. The whole thing looked preposterously spare and antimysterious, like a false front.

The man smiled when I asked for a tapered leader. "Just startin' out, are we?" he said. "You don't need it. You'll do fine with plain old monofilament." And he brought down a spool of what looked to me like purple sewing thread.

"I'd really prefer tapered leader," I said, in the hushed, careful voice of someone asking for groceries in a foreign country. He, in his turn, waved his hand casually in the air, as if my remark were utterly irrelevant.

As I took the monofilament and two locally tied nymphs, he followed me out and told me not to go to that dumb fishing access point—the place'd be crawling with tourists. He drew a spidery, complicated map of a secret hole *no out-of-towners know about*, which I could only get to by trespassing on a local rancher's property. "He doesn't mind," he said, and tipped his hat. As he followed me to the the screen door he added, with a dreamy air, "You'll learn the hard way on that monofilament. Believe me, when you get back to tapered leader, it'll seem like a breeze."

Suffice it to say that though I fished the wrong spot all day, with the wrong line and the wrong fly, the Bitterroot itself, with its willow-shaded margins and islands, its riffles and runs and promising boulders all just out of reach, made failure seem both a reasonable and sublime occupation: ambition, particularly, is a sin against the abiding rush of a river. But I'll confess, I wasn't even in the water when I thought this; I was still standing in the high grass before barbed wire, preparing to crawl between its thorny knots, thinking this was no ordinary fence but the door into the unknown world in all good stories, where spiritual journeys always start. Even the little scratch, the bit of blood on my arm, seemed right and necessary.

This feeling carried me straight through to the next day, north on the Bitterroot highway into Missoula, where, in a slightly clearer but no less literary frame of mind, I found a bona fide fly shop. Of course Missoula has at least a half dozen, all thriving, but this one had a proprietor who, through the big plate windows, bore a striking resemblance to a dear old friend of our family's, Uncle Maury, who in his lifetime had loved fishing and literature with equal passion. He'd point a finger straight up, as if testing the wind, and quote somebody dead—for instance, Jean Cocteau: "The greatest beauty," he'd say, "is the beauty of failure." This made my parents nervous: it was un-American to embrace failure. But he gave me my first great books, among them *Moby-Dick* and Turgenev's *Sketches from a Hunter's Notebook*.

I looked at this owner innocently eating his corned beef sandwich and saw destiny in the coincidence of his familiar bald spot, his heavy glasses, his capable, square-fingered hands. No one else was in the shop for the moment, and when he saw me, he beckoned me in and spoke in a voice as miraculously gruff and East Coast as my old mentor, and took me around to all the cases, shaking his head grimly at my plain old monofilament and box of tattered wet flies while I privately misted over with nostalgia. In real life, I was apparently staring at some little hooks tied with red and gold thread, and he waved his hand disparagingly. "Sure," he said. "That's the San Juan Worm, and it works just fine, but as a beginner, what you really want is a dry fly, so you can see the trout come up for it. That's what'll knock you out."

So I bought from him a half dozen dries, a tapered leader, and some 6X tippet, all the time feeling a kind of warmth spreading in me, a great access of trust, of *home*. He threw in an extra Parachute Adams and a map of Rock Creek with his own favorite spots circled here and there. "Don't fool around up there," he said sternly. "Just stop at the first access point you find." Now, I thought, *now* I'm on track. But as I left the counter, I saw him turn with great comic enthusiasm to two young men who had just entered the shop. To him, I was no hero at all, just one more dazed novice with shaking hands and weak terminology. God only knew what he was telling them now.

Back in the car, I fought the urge to go home, to give up the quest for now. But in my hand I held the map of the next mystery: a world-class fishery I'd never seen. I had the right leader, the right flies, and only twenty-six miles to go. I followed my guide's directions unswervingly. I stopped at the first access point and read the water; I even got my leader a tiny way out. No hits, but it was enough just to know I had tapered leader now, and after a few hours, I was sweetly exhausted by my little progress. The day passed beautifully, uneventfully, in that narrow canyon of building clouds and slate-colored water, a cool wind coming down the valley as the summer took its own first, minute turn toward fall. I'd been there to see it go, and this felt like enough adventure for one day.

It was then, in the cool of late afternoon, in a dark little glade into which leaves dropped with a living patter, that I sat down on my tailgate and set my keys beside me where I could not possibly forget them. I had begun to eat my Wheat Thins when I heard a thrashing in the woods behind me. Into view came a short heavyset man with a red beard, an invader lumbering toward me with spinning rod and cooler. Behind him trailed an ancient, bent woman in giant rubber boots, a long wool skirt, and a kerchief around her head—a dream-babushka straight out of Turgenev's *Sketches*. She had the look of the old crone in fairy tales, the one who delivers the crucial if cryptic message, or opens the right gate, hitherto unnoticed.

But no. The babushka retreated into the forest, and the man lumbered closer. I was pulling off my hip boots when he began to speak in a garbled voice, with an accent deeper than Deep South. He wanted to know how I'd done, what I was using. Parachute Adams, I said. He smirked and sprang the latch on his cooler, where a twenty-inch brown trout lay cramped and faded against the dirty white. He addressed me again in that ferocious accent.

"Juh bring yer bait?" he asked.

"Illegal here," I said coolly.

"It's just un expression," he replied, rolling his eyes a little. "I mean yer bait box with yer Muddler Minners and yer big Woolly Buggers. They're only eatin' the big stuff now, and they're hidin in the troughs. Din't juh notice the eagles?"

I looked politely into the sky, took another Wheat Thin. He rocked on his heels and snapped the cooler shut with a little violence. He was, I suspect, a man who did not like mysteries, particularly.

"Yer fixin' ta leave yer keys," he said, pointing down at my bumper.

I tried to make the best of it, tried to convert this bleak moment as quickly as possible into story. This would be the nadir, this the dragon and the darkest moment of the heroic cycle. But I couldn't; I was depressed as hell. Something about the fading light, the dead fish in the cooler, the reminder, smack in the middle of a lyrical analysis, of the ugly side of failure: the trout lying trapped and flatly dead between his condescending teachings and my stubborn ignorance. It was too dark to go back out into the river again, and he stood there, quite clearly waiting to see me leave, as if he'd been sent to take up the last available light. The river was aloof now, cool and secretive, no risers, not a ripple in the troughs, the eagles gone up to their roosts.

"Well, I better get goin'," he said. "Don't forget them keys."

I waited there until I could no longer hear his boots crushing the brittle leaves, until I could no longer see his white cooler, that awful beacon, floating backward through the darkening woods. When it was quiet, I got back in the car and headed out Rock Creek Road, back toward Missoula. But I couldn't believe the story was over, so bleakly, hopelessly, finished. I was starved for a better ending. And lo, as if in answer, there rose up before me the Rock Creek Fly Shop, which, in my haste to get streamside, I'd missed on the way in. At the very least, I told myself, just use the bathroom, grab a soda, ask what these guys would have used.

I stumbled in, Eve expelled from the river for not knowing that the trout were lying in the troughs because of eagles, and eatin' only Muddler Minners. I nodded at the man behind the counter and tried to look like I knew my way around, but I couldn't see a rest-room door anywhere.

"Lady," he said. "If it had teeth it would jump up and bite you."

"Just tell me where it is," I said tensely.

He pointed behind me.

When I came out of the rest room, he smiled. "You look tired," he said. "What were you using—I hear they're pulling in the big browns like nobody's business!" I shook my head and he slapped his hands on the counter. "You were using *what?*" he said. "What joker told you to use a dry on a day like this?" He paused dramatically, hand on the phone, ready to dial 911. "It's only big stuff now, they're only eatin' big stuff." Again, the sad shake of the head, the unspoken message that if I'd only asked him first instead of the Guys in Town, I'd be rich with fish— hell, Missoula's twenty-six miles away, what do they know?

It occurred to me that I should stop taking advice for a while, that all advice was suspect, hopelessly rooted in some deep and complicated tangle of pride and secret regret that rose up to meet the susceptible customer with her own deep and complicated tangle of pride and secret regret.

But the proprietor had stopped talking, and was looking at me as if I'd asked him a deep theological question. "Wait a minute," he said. "Come with me." He beckoned me away from the counter and the cases of flies, around a corner to another room entirely—one I would never have guessed was there. In this room a potbellied woodstove hissed and crackled. A family was seated around the stove: two brothers in red flannel shirts and jeans were cleaning their guns; a young woman, with cheeks flushed from the heat of the stove, was knitting; a baby, also red-faced, with its knitted cap fallen low over one eye, lay regal and stunned in its swaddling.

The proprietor seated himself at a round table piled high with yarn, feathers, fur, and thread. "Here we go," he said. He wound red chenille around the shank of a hook and burned both ends with a match. "I call it the Poor Man's San Juan Worm," he said. "It has no class, but when all else fails—"

I didn't leave right away. I held myself still, welcomed, if not into the life of the river, then a step closer to it. It was like falling into a fine old painting of peasant life, where there's sunlight drifting down from some window you can't see. The dog sleeps, the hunters pause over their guns, the baby lies amazed under the golden light. We are at the beginning again, with Rock Creek just outside, moving swiftly through its canyon as the dark comes on in earnest. Cocteau would approve, and so would Uncle Maury: by failing to catch trout, look at the gift you've been granted.

Never mind that on my next visit to Missoula, the owner of the fly shop there would look at my San Juan Worm and say accusingly, "Where the hell did you get this? It's all wrong. Who made it?" My host at Rock Creek must have known this would happen, because as he handed me the finished fly, he smiled the brief, cramped smile of the failed artist, the wise teacher.

"Just a little present," he said. "Since you tried so hard. Just promise me you won't tell the guys in Missoula who made it. They'd have my head."

FLORESTAN AND EUSEBIUS

Somewhere in a box of old family photos there's one of my father and his best friend, Maury Rudens, as medical students in Chicago. It's the early 1930s, and by some accident of age or photography, they are surrounded by a nimbus of light. They look priestly in their white tunics, and here, in their late twenties, with their receding hairlines and spectacles, they are already hard to tell apart. They're squinting into the sun, but it looks like something more to me, as if they are amazed by their good luck so far, and want us to be, too. A dreamed-of arrival has been accomplished, a frontier, and they hold themselves still in a moment of possibility, before the next departure.

I can't find this picture now, and it haunts me like a death. It has vanished, like my father and Uncle Maury, only to come back in dreams and imagination. My yearning for this photograph has, I think, something to do with the need to see them young, since by the time I was ten they were already in their fifties and old to me, less father and friend than a pair of eccentric grandfather-twins from a nineteenth-century Russian novel, always arguing over books or politics. They sealed this mystery for life by dying within a year of each other, both of leukemia. I was nineteen at the time, but somewhere in the back of my mind, behind grief and confusion, I had the consoling illusion that they'd arranged it, composing, up to the last minute, the drama of their lives together.

My father would tell me I'm a crackpot. Enough with the theories. Probably they inhaled the same toxic fumes back in medical school. Maury would object, too, but for other reasons. "Life is more complicated than any of us knows," he'd say, his voice all aggravation and wonder. "You want the real story? Read Chekhov, read Tolstoy."

This is the way it was with them: throughout my childhood their voices played against each other in uneven counterpoint. My father took the part of practicality and reason, of plot lines rising straight to a dramatic crisis. His was the melody of the self-made man, while Maury wavered like a shadow-brother at his side, syncopating, mocking, changing the key. Sometimes he'd simply wait till my father was busy or taking a rest, then put into my hands a famous old novel— quickly, with a rapid glance over his shoulder, as if through it he meant to tell me the true story of our family's life.

How Maury came to play such a central role in our lives is the first question. Hazy myth is all I've got, along with my own invented images of Chicago in the twenties and thirties: gangsters and nickel movie houses, my father a skinny kid with a bum leg from the polio—Charlie Chaplin and Horatio Alger all at once—gazing up at a divine dream between shabby velvet curtains. I like to imagine him meeting Maury in such a place, finding his double in a dark room where only the essence of drama and its promise mattered. My mother says it was nothing so glamorous; she's pretty sure they met later, in a required college English course. *Pretty sure*. I depend on her uncertainty.

What I know is this: my father grew up a sickly Jewish boy in a tough Chicago neighborhood, in a couple of rooms above his father's Hungarian printing press. His mother made huge, heavy meals to fatten up her boy; he stayed skinny no matter what. How many times did he almost die? The polio, the scarlet fever, the influenza of 1918 . . . with a wave of his hand he brushed death aside: it was not his fate to succumb. His stories were briefly, hotly drawn, a series of fabulous cartoon frames rapidly passing. Ghetto boy makes good, gets scholarship to college, medical school. Enemies are vanquished, one by one, before the listening child can, God forbid, interrupt to ask about an errant detail.

But Maury's life had the grainy texture, the murky dark of domestic life missing in my father's grand tales—was it part of my father's escape to leave such details out? I wanted for my father Uncle Maury's mantel clock, with its oppressive ticking in the quiet parlor; the gleam of Professor Ruden's gramophone in the corner of the room. Pipe tobacco, chicken broth, something faintly sinister in the medicinal air. Maury came from a different world, even if it was only a few blocks away: his parents were cultured people, German Jewish refugees, his father a university professor of Jewish history, the patriarch I'd know later in Kafka's stories, that paralyzing figure of authority in an old dressing gown. "Maury worshiped the old man," my mother used to say, lowering her voice. "But he must have been hell to live with. You know, his wife wound up in an institution."

This felt like the real thing: urgent, awful, a tale of imprisonment and longed-for escape. Did I betray my father? I should have been holding my breath in high suspense for the moment he knocked the local bully flat in the alley behind Clybourn Avenue. I didn't. I ached for the boy in the professor's parlor to get away.

But I was growing up in a parlor myself—the careful suburbs of postwar California—where the story of my father's big American journey couldn't sprout, and there I waited for some more convincing drama, something more slippery and ruinous, set not in a big city but in a kitchen, a darkened living room like our own. I listened carefully for a clue, but nothing drove it up in the tricky music between them. There was only Maury's high disgust at my father's moneymaking schemes and enthusiasm for the Dow-Jones, sung against my father's disdain for Maury's old dream of being a novelist. "You can't raise a family on a writer's income; for God's sake, even

Saul Bellow can't do it," my father liked to say. And so, with only a little provocation, I decided that my father had discouraged Maury from fulfilling his dream by making him come to medical school. The irony horrified me and made perfect sense: Maury was a bachelor, after all, and had no family, unless you counted us. Was it our fault he didn't write? For by then we had come to call him Uncle Maury. He was our extra father, the man who stood in when ours was distant, melancholy, or just too busy.

Maury had a penchant for literature of the previous century, for nostalgists and procrastinators and mad artists who stepped out of the fast current. He loved to refer to my father as a fictional character, an act I believed to be his secret revenge. "He's a regular Karenin," he'd say grimly, raising his eyebrows. "Someday you'll know what I mean." He would tantalize me thus, with books I wasn't old enough to read; the possible answer lay available, but not quite, waiting for me to hurry up and grow. When would I?

What I got, while I was waiting, was a nice literary confusion about life. My father and Maury are inseparable now, like the doubles who dominate the tales of E. T. A. Hoffman, who figure in Dostoyevsky, Poe, and Hawthorne. Ivan Turgenev once said that all men were either Hamlet or Quixote—men of thought or men of action. In this symmetry my father is Don Quixote, of course, with his mad tilting at financial windmills, uranium mines in Nevada, broasted-chicken franchises, and once, when I was eleven, a rock-and-roll band. He woke me early that morning and brought me into the living room. "Some outfit called Poco is going public," he said and, to my astonishment, put an album on the turntable. "Whaddya think?" he said. "Should I snap up forty shares?" I had no idea what he meant, but my heart beat fast. "I guess they're okay," I said carefully. "Well then," he replied. "I'd better get on the horn to New York." This happened, as did all his big communications, in the dark of six A.M., the hour the stock exchange opened in New York, and just before he went off to his medical office.

It's harder to say when Maury practiced medicine, for when he wasn't arguing with my father or trying to get him out on the half-day boat for some albacore fishing, he was in our kitchen, talking to my mother about the lives of the great composers. Talking, talking; I see him now, the mad insomniac of Turgenev's "Hamlet of the Shchigrovsky District," a man of great possibilities who cannot decide what to do, how to make his mark, though he feels, immensely, that he has a mark to make; a man who does not even grant himself "the bitter pleasure of irony—after all, there's no such thing as irony in isolation."

No irony in isolation. Was this why, when he came to our house, he was full of wordplay and clever, bitter commentary on the world? It might be that his bachelor solitude repeated the solitude of his childhood, that place surely too tight for irony, for the light and air of argument, that place where he was captive under the weight of his father's certainty. With my father and our family, he at least had a chance to fight and be heard, to *breathe*, for though my father's worldly success was impossible to beat, Maury knew literature, music, history. My father could not best him in the world of art and culture. He knew something more, too, I think: my father's sad and child-like self, how starved for company he was, and how awkward he was when he got it. None of us children knew this—we only felt it, each in a different way, that kingly absence deep at the root of our lives.

Whatever it was that composed my father's loneliness we cannot know, only that Maury, with his marvelous high irrita-tion with the world, sometimes saved him from facing it. He saved all of us, so fully that for a long time I never considered that he might have a life without us. I only knew that when he was gone, there was something wrong with our house, an im-balance nobody could correct.

He did live somewhere, of course, though as a child I wasn't allowed to see his apartment—another enticing gap opened up here. My mother would go so far as to tell me it was "somewhere in West Los Angeles, a terrible place, a dump." My father would quickly add, "He's a doctor, for God's sake, what's he doing living in the slums?" But Maury insisted on staying there, giving me another inadvertent gift: the im-age of a sordid room above Sunset Boulevard, lit by pulsing neon—GIRLS, GIRLS, GIRLS—that cast its fiendish, alluring imprint on an old mattress. Books everywhere: on rickety shelves to the ceiling, in heaps on the kitchen table. Beside the mattress was the thing itself, the box of typescript he'd once told me about. It was a novel, he'd said, a hopeless enterprise. "Melville spoiled that game long ago," he said. "Nobody can ever write the great American novel after *Moby-Dick*."

Whatever else I was wrong about, I was right about the books, for after a big earthquake in the late sixties, he was nearly buried in them. It was, my mother said, because of the earthquake that he came to live with us for a time, bringing with him his most loved books. I was twelve, and I remember only that he unpacked them the way someone might unpack his grandparents' heirlooms from the old country, kneeling, explaining, delicately holding them forth as though they were ancient, breakable things. Until this time, books had had no such sacredness about them, though we were, by southern California standards, a bookish family. They were reckless boarders in our house. My father's books were purely that, my father's books, living in our bookshelves in an eclectic mix, the worthy and the dubious flung together in no particular order, like a man's jumbled memories of his life. Wartime paperbacks leaned against the romantic adventures of *Two Years Before the Mast* and *Green Mansions*, next to Leon Uris, Daphne du Maurier, H. Rider Haggard, and a growing collection of rare medical texts. His favorite book was *The Story of San Michele*, written by Axel Munthe, a Swedish doctor who lived for a time on the island of Capri, restoring the ruined villa of the Emperor Tiberius and working among the villagers. At my father's funeral, one of my brothers would read a passage from this book, in which Munthe prepares himself for his own death. It is an elevated bit of prose and reads sentimentally to me now, but there is power in it, when I think of my father and listen again: "Happiness we can only find in ourselves, it is a waste of time to seek for it from others, few have any to spare." But it is elsewhere in the book that I hear what my father yearned for: a big life full of travel and change and flashes of medical heroism in remote places. How odd and right it seems that Munthe calls himself "Quixottish" and, in a chapter called "Insomnia," invents for himself a doppelgänger, a shadow-self, to argue with.

It is also right—and in character—that my father would wait until after his own death to speak through a book, through yet another child who ached to know him. And it is equally right that Maury wouldn't be able to *stop* talking through books until his. He would hold an obscure volume in his hand and look at me with an expression I couldn't interpret, somewhere between joy and judgment. It jolted me, even as a child, with the certainty that herein lay the *one* significant thing. I must not, under any condition, let it go.

The summer he lived with us, he began to buy me books. The first was one of my father's favorites—one of the few of which Maury approved—*The Adventures of Augie March*. He beckoned me into the guest room and sat me down. "Your first Saul Bellow," he said. "You'll probably never recover." These new books smelled utterly fresh, the ink driven deeper into the page than in my father's old paperbacks, which now seemed like lower-class cousins. I liked to run my finger across the satiny chocolate brown sticker from Vroman's in Pasadena. Receiving these, I felt like a character in a book myself, a book about a young girl who will grow up and surprise everyone . . .

Proust, Tolstoy, E. T. A. Hoffman. Dostoyevsky, *that brilliant slob*. And looming above them all, the formidable figure of Melville. "I'm giving you *Moby-Dick* now," he said. "You're too young, but what the hell." I remember holding the great book in my hands and deciding, very deliberately, not to read it until I was sixteen. I rocked with it in my rocker and turned its pages with luxuriant pleasure, pretending to be a grown-up reader. It was, I think now, a kind of reading.

But I'd be well past sixteen when I finally read *Moby-Dick*, or anything else he gave me, for secretly, compulsively, I was reading trash. Historical romance novels with glistening covers and titles suggesting illicit pairings: *The Wolf and the Dove*, *The Flame and the Flower*. My favorite was *The Green Darkness*, a huge saga of reincarnated lovers—I scorned my father's books and was just like him, with the literary taste of a Hungarian peasant. A real Philistine.

Surely Maury knew my wretched habit, and ignored it, for he needed badly to talk, and be listened to. I hid my bad-girl books under the bed, dimly sensing they would hurt his finer sensibilities and make him lose confidence in me. I loved nothing more than to see him hold his fiery glass of bourbon high in the air and cry out, "What American could hope to write anything after *Moby-Dick*? What's the goddamned point?" His passion, with its nagging distress beneath, frightened and exhilarated me. It spoke of a story under the story, and another under that, like a series of underground caves. I believed him with the terrified wholeheartedness of twelve, and loved literature so he would reveal the secret to me.

But it was not there, *not* among books, that I began to think I had discovered the real story at last. There was a third voice running through—how hadn't I heard it before? It was my mother's, and so had to emerge through the subject of music, and in our kitchen, where my father's power was diminished. There Maury could infiltrate, could cajole and tease and talk to her endlessly in a language my father couldn't speak. Literature didn't exactly work, so he concentrated on the merits and failures of certain composers. Rachmaninoff he particularly could not abide, and some Tchaikovsky. But Prokofiev's *Romeo and Juliet*, anything by Shostakovich, and Brahms—ah Brahms, what a genius. . . . He fought with her on the subject of Mozart versus Bach, melody or mathematics—did she want the genius of pathos or the genius of the cold stars? Who, at twelve, could hear a man talking to her mother so passionately and not think it? I watched her face change, saw a light and mobility come over it, inexplicably, as she cut carrots for the relish tray and he tried to undo the laces of her unbudging preference for Bach. She held him off, but it was too late. I had *seen*. It was as if he'd exposed, through her musical taste, what lay beneath her monastic attention to domestic detail. Yet, though she sparred with him and laughed in a way I'd never heard before, she revealed nothing graspable, only grew more unknowable and interesting as she performed her endless rituals at sink and stove. I waited for one of them to make a mistake, to say something off the subject and in a low, urgent tone, but it did not come. He stood, always held back from her by the barrier of the kitchen island she herself had designed, with its diner-style counter on one side and her stove on the other, in what I came to see as the eternal delay of true love.

I want to say that this is it, the story I was looking for, but I can't, exactly, for my mother's part remained hidden. Maury moved back into a place of his own, though he visited faithfully every Saturday. On those days, late in the afternoon, when they'd been talking for hours and I thought it was certain—my God, they loved each other and were forbidden—she'd turn from the stove and look beyond Maury, beyond all the windows of our house. She'd point toward the living room, where my father lay napping on the couch. "Maury," she'd say. "I need a little peace and quiet. Go bug *him*—and take *her* with you"—for I'd begun to take after Maury and was becoming a talker, too. Maury would bow his head in a courtly way and signal me to come along.

So we were exiled into my father's domain, the living room where he lay on the couch, laid low by one of his new headaches, by the gout, by a tough week at the office. He lay there, his hands folded across his chest like a pharaoh in his final repose, an imposing monument to actual, unromanticized fatherhood. No matter what he did or didn't do, he remained the real father—a condition, it must have seemed to Maury, bestowed on him by a God bent on cruelest irony. "Charles Bovary himself," he'd hiss tenderly, standing over my father's prone form. "He's a goddamned Philistine, your pater, but how can you not love him, the son of a bitch."

While my father slept, or pretended to, Maury went on. He called him "a musical peasant." Did I know my father loved "schmaltz?" I did. His favorite song was "Lara's Theme" from *Doctor Zhivago*, with its tremulous balalaikas strumming as the camera slowly pans across the vast snowy steppes. Maybe a secret romantic was lodged in my father's innermost heart, but he was hampered, and could only make a little joke of his lonely, passionate nature. He would sometimes approach the family piano and pick out the theme in a childlike halting way. Even this was too much for him. He'd roll quickly into his other "piece," a terrible, jaunty polka: *When I went to Germany, all the girls were stuck on me. One was blind and the other couldn't see, when I went to Ger-man-y.*

Maury posed himself elegantly against this primitive background, in plain view of my musical mother, to no avail. As I entered my midteens, she was less and less available for "musical discussion," as he called it, and I took over as his chief listener, accompanist to something, or nothing—I'd never know. When I was fifteen and at the peak of my romantic suspicions, his favorite composer was Robert Schumann, the most hectically passionate of all. I can't remember any musical analysis, only the human drama: he seemed to know Robert and Clara intimately, as well as their young friend Johannes Brahms. He'd play recordings of Schumann's *Carnaval*, and point out the little phrase at the top: *dedicated to Clara by Florestan and Eusebius, Opus 11*. These two characters, he explained, were the two sides of Schumann's musical personality: Florestan was the passionate idealist, full of ideas and action, and Eusebius was the pale-browed introvert, a Hamlet forever considering the consequences of any action. Never mind that Clara was only twelve at the time, a brilliant young pianist and his own teacher's daughter. Florestan and Eusebius would be with Schumann his whole life, straight through to the depths of the madness that killed him—as Clara was destined to be, too.

"A genius, a madman," said Maury. "Robert married Clara against her father's wishes, gave her eight children, and ruined her career." Then he gave me his sober, enthralling look. "Listen, kid. This happens to great women all the time. Don't make the same mistake."

Maybe he was waiting for me to ask, finally, what he really meant, to beg for the storyteller's story. But I was fifteen, greedy for high drama, for the culminating scene in the Schumann family drama. One night, it seems, near the end of his life and at the height of his madness, Schumann heard in his sleep the most divine music—it seemed to be coming to him from the great composers of the past. He struggled out of bed to write down the notes, which he knew to be the greatest composition of his life, but as he took up his pen, the notes turned suddenly demonic, a hellish cacophony built of the same stuff. He fled the house and ran to the banks of the Rhine, where he flung himself into the water. He was discovered almost immediately by passing fishermen and rescued. The terrible irony, Maury said, was that it happened to be Carnival time, and as the fishermen carried him home through the festive midnight streets, revelers mistook the group for street players, and applauded wildly as they passed.

But Maury wasn't finished. Did I know that the Schumanns' young friend Brahms had a terrible crush on Clara, and that during the final days of Schumann's life, they struggled to conceal their growing passion for each other? After Schumann's death, they never got together, he said. Nobody knows why, for she threw most of their correspondence into the waters of the Rhine. Who cares, said Maury. It's better that way, as a story of unrequited love, didn't I agree?

He stopped the story there, leaving his own alive and ever-widening in my mind. Who was he, this man trapped somewhere between two visions of his place with us: was he our Scheherazade, staying Death's hand with endless story, or the interloper, waiting for the husband to die?

Sometime in the early seventies, he vanished briefly out of our lives, like some private Odysseus, while our family wove and unwove the tapestry of our awkward middle years. The last of my brothers went on to college, and my parents and I moved to a beach town fifty miles south of Los Angeles. This new house, built on an ocean cliff, was even quieter than our old one; I could hear our family's silence, absolutely, against the lonely surge of the Pacific. I suspect now that Maury was not gone at all, but that my parents, in the midst of their own quiet marital distress, wanted no witness. But at the time I only knew that there were long stretches without Maury in them, a loss of symmetry in our life. Without him, we'd come unhinged. He must have been traveling part of the time: post-cards came from Israel, Egypt, and even Japan. Then one night he telephoned to say that he was a married man.

At first my mother didn't believe it. She came away from the telephone looking pale. "He married a dancer in Las Vegas," she said to my father, cupping her hand over the receiver as she handed it to him. For years after, I believed that he'd married a Las Vegas showgirl, a stripper. She was, in fact, his instructor of ballroom dancing, right there in Los Angeles. This is infi-nitely more lifelike, but it was not in my interest to see it at the time. I was still devouring ruinous fantasy set between soft covers, with their voluptuous females yearning upward into the arms of strangers. My eye was trained on the sordid and precarious—only these possibilities counted.

Her name was Penny, and when I finally met her, she was a terrible disappointment: a tall, bony divorcée with white-blond hair and a small nervous dog who accompanied her everywhere. Her only saving grace, in my harsh view, was her teenaged son. Gordon had long brown hair that fell in his eyes, and slim shaky fingers like mine. I watched him covertly when they came to visit, a dark ticking in my arms and legs. Once we all traveled together, to my oldest brother's engagement party in San Francisco, and spent the night in a suite of rooms at a Chinatown hotel. Of that place I remember only the red-lit lobby with its statue of a Chinese goddess, and a big bed into which you could drop quarters to start it wildly rocking. Gordon put in a quarter and we lay down, side by side, holding ourselves perfectly rigid while the bed shook and jiggled us. At last Penny stood in the doorway, her hand over her mouth in terror. Maybe she was already afraid of losing her fragile relationship with Maury; surely she knew how he much he lived under my parents' potent sway. And, in fact, within a few years they were living apart, and Maury spoke of her only bitterly. "What a mistake, what a nightmare." And Gordon too vanished from our lives.

But Maury was back with us, leaning over the kitchen counter and talking compulsively until, as my mother told me years later, she was wild with boredom. So I began to see that he wasn't the great hidden love of her life, either. Was anyone? Just as I was ready to consider the possible disappointments of her life, disappointment no longer mattered. My father was diagnosed with acute leukemia, and told he had nine months to live.

Then one night there was another phone call, and my mother's face was pale again, as she cupped her hand over the receiver in her old way and handed the phone to my father.

"It's Maury," she said. "He's sick too." My father nodded and took the call in another room. At the time this could mean only one thing to me: that Maury had contracted a gruesome venereal disease from all his wild living. Not until after both Maury and my father were dead would my mother tell me that Maury had, like him, been diagnosed with leukemia, though the chronic kind, she said, not the acute. He had made my parents promise not to tell anyone; he thought he might last awhile.

So it was that the year my father fought his cancer dramatically, flying to special clinics back East and reading all the latest medical journals—a true Quixote at last—Maury kept his own diagnosis a secret. Maury, the nonstop talker, the man who could make a kid believe there was nothing greater in the world than a certain passage in Proust or a couple of measures from a Mozart piano concerto, refused to say that he was dying too.

My father was no Schumann, and Maury no Brahms. Who is Florestan, without his Eusebius? Maury could not, finally, wrestle his life story into shape. It clunked, the way life will just when you most need the story of it.

I don't remember seeing him at my father's funeral, though my mother says this is ridiculous, of course he was there. But the memory is unaccountably stubborn. And so my last recollection of him comes from a moment long before the real end, from the early days of my father's illness, before I knew exactly what was wrong. It was a Sunday night, and

Maury had offered to take me out to dinner. I heard him discussing it with my mother in the kitchen, asking if he could help by "getting the kid out of the house for a couple hours." My mother sighed, relieved. I didn't understand—I was insulted and elated all at once.

In Wong's Paradise Maury ordered a bourbon and started in on Melville. "*Moby-Dick*," he said. "Did I ever tell you I once tried to write the great American novel?"

I shook my head as if this was news to me—this was our ritual. I asked him if he still had his manuscript somewhere.

"Oh, I think it's in an old box somewhere, among the rats," he said, but he glanced away awkwardly, and for the first time it occurred to me that he might be lying, that the manuscript might not exist at all. I looked away, and felt him eye me sharply. "You're not still thinking about being a writer, are you? Forget it, kid. Melville spoiled the game long ago."

The food came, and we fell into a strained silence. It was suddenly like being with my father, in the strange hollow of those last few years, when I knew only that he wanted me to do better in school and not go out with "such rotten characters." I couldn't look at Maury now, afraid of that silence coming from him. He looked away too, and the whole world went quiet.

But then I looked where he looked, toward the restaurant's bar. A young waiter was drying glasses methodically, giving each one a beautiful final twist with a white towel. I began to watch with interest.

"Look at that kid," Maury said. "His family just got to America, and already he wants to be an engineer. He's putting himself through school. If you looked behind the bar, I bet you'd see his big textbooks."

I nodded and kept watching, and, as if it were a scene Maury was writing while we sat there, the boy lifted a big textbook up onto the bar and opened it. The new silence heightened everything. I saw, for the first time, what my father's hands might have looked like once, young and smooth and serious, the fingers lightly drumming on his first medical textbook. It wasn't the great American novel that glimmered there but a stark, simple tale by Chekhov. In that doubled silence, Maury's and my father's, I saw how thin and cheap the waiter's white shirt was, how it revealed, barely, the skin beneath and the sad outline of his undershirt. I saw the array of pens stuck in the shirt pocket. The chest again, so thin and bony. Did he eat anything besides rice? Would he make it to engineering school?

Maury was looking at me—severely, I thought—but this time I didn't look away.

"Listen, kid," he said. "Back there, a few minutes ago, what I said about Melville—I didn't mean it. What the hell. Go ahead and give it a try. Your father would want it too."

Ever since their deaths, and since I can't find the old photograph again, I keep another picture on my work desk, a strange substitute for the lost one. It's a blurry copy of the last photograph ever taken of the great Russian Jewish writer Isaac Babel. I keep it there to remind myself of Babel's honesty and the Chagall-like wildness of his metaphors, but the truth is, his face reminds me of Maury's and my father's from before I was born: a light in the eyes, an amazement about life. From the caption, we learn that Babel is about to be exiled to Siberia for reasons unknown. He will die there, silenced at the height of his powers. After this moment, no more words will come from this man who once wrote, "The world was beautiful, just to give us pleasure." But in the photograph he is at peace, leaning forward in his chair, gazing at the photographer, and in his eyes is that unearthly light, composed of resignation and humor and wisdom all at once. He is beyond Siberia, beyond Stalin and politics and the disappointments of the profane world, beyond his own death, and ours. His mouth is closed and faintly smiling, as if he's just finished speaking. What did he say? I want to know, and can't. That's the pain and pleasure of reading him, Maury would say if he were here. The brief golden sentences drop so fast, you might miss them altogether—or be dazzled for life, depending.

ATTITUDE CREEK

I've taken the enthusiastic advice of the young man at the Dan Bailey Flyfishing Shop in Livingston, Montana, and am headed up to Slough Creek, his favorite spot, and Yellowstone's best-kept secret. "All the other rivers are jammed," he said. "But Slough Creek's a bit of a trek; most people don't like to work that hard." This sounded good at the time, though I was faintly suspicious: why would anyone reveal the location of his favorite stretch of river, or any best-kept secret? But I was past the point of cool analysis. My husband was babysitting our daughter; I had the family car. I had my brother's old fly rod and hip boots and a box full of delicate flies sold to me by shop owners across the state who appeared to wish me well. And if nothing else, I'd have solitude.

Before I left the shop the young man offered further advice; it got complex, and his voice got passionate, gained authority. "Drop a nymph on 'em," he said. "A Gold-Ribbed Hare's Ear, with a split-shot or two." Next thing I knew, I'd purchased three at two bucks a pop, plus a tiny expensive box of minute non-toxic split-shot, for which I would need the steady fingers of a neurosurgeon, or at least privacy, lest an experienced fisherman spot me fumbling the simplest of operations.

The winding washboard road just past Tower Junction seems a good sign I'll have the place to myself—the road is too small for RVs, too bumpy for Yellowstone's jogging-suit-and-binoculars set. But mysteriously, at its conclusion, there are fifty parked cars. Chargers, Broncos, Samurais: serious vehicles, lined up in the meadow and coated with a fine layer of dirt, as if to announce they've been here a long time—a lot longer than my small white hatchback, anyway. But the meadow is quiet: maybe these sportsmen have gone downstream, or so deep into the backcountry that I'll never see them.

I sign in at the trail register, fingers trembling, as if by going fishing alone I am doing something sneaky or rebellious, maybe even illicit. Sure enough, the notice over the register reads: DON'T HIKE ALONE: YOU ARE IN BEAR COUNTRY. For a moment I'd forgotten. As I'd left the house, my husband had told me thirteen grizzly anecdotes, and had our mild-natured little girl springing out at me from corners, growling.

"Remember," he said. "When in doubt, play dead."

His going-away present was a thirty-dollar can of pepper spray, the extralarge, he added, frowning at me with that potent mix of tenderness and fatherly mistrust that has stunned me into obedience all my life. What impulse made me tuck the can deep in my vest's back pocket, where I could never reach it in time, even if I had the steady fingers of a neurosurgeon?

Two hikers walk up while I'm signing my name and destination in the trail register, and with what I hope is proper etiquette, I ask if I might hike behind them, as to be safe from bears. The man is fully outfitted for fly fishing; the woman, not. But it is the woman who looks at me with exasperated goodwill. She says brusquely, "Don't worry. There aren't any bears up here."

They suffer me to walk behind them the two miles up to Slough Creek. Dutifully, I stop at twenty paces every time they do, which is often: to photograph wildflowers, vistas, and finally a doe and her two fawns trying to find a quiet place to browse. My sympathies are with the doe, who just wants to forage in peace, but who eventually gives up on the notion and poses for a shot before bounding delicately away.

When Slough Creek comes at last into view, so do the owners of the Chargers, Broncos, and Samurais. Figures in re-galia punctuate the lush high grass and kneel over the cutbank in various postures of worship. In the great meadow, women sit in the tall grass reading or painting with little watercolor sets. The atmosphere, though overlaid with the deep incessant buzz of greenhead flies and mosquitoes, is as hushed as any sanctuary.

Then I notice that these fishermen are not using nymphs. No, all of them, down to the last man, are casting the tiniest, most delicate of dry flies. But the young man at Dan Bailey's said nymphs, and I've paid good money for nymphs, so, damn it, I'll use nymphs. I find a spot equidistant between two fishermen, tie on the Gold-Ribbed Hare's Ear, and, after some struggle, two of the tiny weights. In a sorry imitation of the professionals around me, I fall to my knees and inch up to the bank, where I look down and find myself gazing straight into that which does require worship: clear slow water, bright red and gray and black stones, and big cutthroats lined up nose-to-tail for all to see. Trembling again, I tenderly lower my rod, and let my offering drift down among these beautiful trout.

Almost immediately, there is a shadow on the water. I turn to find a fisherman looming. He neither smiles nor nods; his expression is austere, his forehead permanently creased from the ardors of long spiritual search. "Let me guess," he says, sighing. "You're dropping a nymph on him." And then, as if to reinforce his stern judgment, a stitch of lightning rends the western sky; deep rumbling follows. "Try a little dry, maybe a number-eighteen Elk-Hair Caddis," he says, squinting at the clouds. "And don't get yourself killed."

Ultimately, the gods are kind: before the storm hits, I discover, further upstream, a long meander inhabited by only one other fisherman. Inspired by this relative privacy, I follow the expert's advice and tie on an Elk-Hair Caddis. Three casts later, there is a silver flash on the water, a slurp, and I am granted the secret shock of connection. Forget bears and experts and lightning; forget fear of failure. As I bring in a handsome cutthroat, admire it, and release it, the fisherman below me inclines his head ever so slightly. Then, as if this small triumph was frankly too much, lightning strikes deep in the meadow and everybody, expert and novice alike, seeks shelter under the big firs.

After the thunderstorm, there are suddenly more fishermen on the water. And the atmosphere has changed; morning services are over and everyone's at the local pub for a pint. The purists have vanished utterly, or metamorphosed into big friendly chaps. This new crowd doesn't bother to crouch on the bank; everyone is wading, laughing, convivial. Emboldened by my little victory and this cheery atmosphere, I find a spot to wade in; the only opening is at the end of a lineup of five men and their guide.

Then, from among the men, there is a sudden hoarse bark of joy, a post-touchdown outburst. It seems all wrong, and the silence in the meadow deepens all around it, as if to isolate the man who made it. The four others and the guide are murmuring congratulations to the man who has caught the big trout, who keeps hooting as he plays the fish and brings it to splash heavily at his feet. The others shift uncomfortably, and move a few feet away from him. The big winner doesn't notice. He keeps laughing, shouting now as he holds up his net, the fish thrashing and sinking; he makes the guide admire it before he lets it go. Five minutes later, it happens again, then again. The guide smiles mournfully in my direction.

"Somebody's having a good day," he says, as if by bringing the man here he, too, has sinned.

I hear it, and realize that this is what I should have dreaded all along—not company, not condescension, not death by grizzly. The meadow and creek seem to hold still, but nothing happens. There is no divine retribution, either in the form of lightning or sudden prophets. Secretly, I am afraid that I myself, as a newcomer to this creek and the whole complicated art of fly fishing, am capable of such a noise.

For the rest of the afternoon, I use nymphs, in full knowledge that the trout will not want them. It's the only gesture I can think of, somehow: an homage to the Slough Creek that must have once been somebody's favorite spot, and Yellowstone's best-kept secret. At times like these, deliberate failure is a way of keeping yourself from feeling like an accomplice. By midafternoon the trout have stopped rising and I am glad. Nothing breaks the glassy surface; Slough Creek has taken its secrets back. Even the big winner is quiet, defeated, finally, by the enigmas of habitat.

I walk the two miles back to the car unchaperoned. To hell with the rules, with the grizzlies, with the dangers of lone hiking. Deep in the woods now, away from Slough Creek, I feel a kind of peace seeping back in; I'm on the verge of regaining the thing I came for, which maybe isn't precisely solitude, but a moment of unremarked, unannounced partnership with the wilderness. Alone, I've at least got my tremble back, and it's not about illicit departures anymore, but the hope that comes from standing at the gates of the kingdom we abandoned so long ago, and are always running from. I want to step further in—something in me is longing for the grizzly, a sort of private judgment day. Or so I am thinking when there is a terrible crash in the brush beside me. I freeze.

It's the doe again, with her two fawns. She looks up with marvelous calm and the two fawns venture closer. While I hold still, they commence to nose the bracken, looking now for supper, then briefly at me, then for supper again. They are waiting for me to leave, to stop staring while they eat. The doe lifts her head slightly, and I bow mine, thinking as I do that I wish people didn't have to make such a big deal out of a walk in the woods, a visit to a stream.

But we do.

WAITING FOR A MIRACLE:
A JEW GOES FISHING

One Saturday morning, waist deep in the Colorado River, I glanced up to see a dozen Hasids in long black coats and fedoras standing on the bridge above me. I closed my eyes to dismantle this hallucination, but when I opened them the Hasids were still there, gazing down at me, mournfully stroking their beards. I made a cast—into the trees. I made another and missed a strike. The men frowned and moved on, but it was too late: I knew myself judged. What kind of chutzpah was this, a Jew trying to walk in harmony with nature? And in the water, no less, that famous Christian element. Is there a posture in the world that smacks more of the desire for premature transcendence than this business of standing midstream, trying to raise fishes from the deep?

All day I felt my klutziness—my absolute fishlessness—like a curse; I wondered idly if there was a prohibition against fishing on the Sabbath. Before this, I'd figured myself the usual beginner with a long way to go, but that day, watched by smart trout below and wise Jews above, I began to think I wasn't fated to improve. What if I wasn't so much a bad fisherman as a person struggling hopelessly against an ancient tribal destiny?

On the other hand, what were a bunch of pious Jews doing on a western riverbank on a Sabbath morning, gazing down at an angler and the water too, their pallid faces bearing the expression of fishermen everywhere: that absorbed, childlike alertness, everything in the world forgotten but the river and what might lie beneath its surface? Surely they'd come further than any fisherman to stand on the bank of this river, which suddenly, under a passing cloud, turned that promising greeny-gray that says *trout* to some people, but by saying so, speaks to the mysteries we all wait for: divine before you see it, mortal when you do.

The smallest, most idle speculation kept tugging at me, right through summer and into fall, a thousand miles from a brief humiliation on the trout stream. Maybe it's the academic life. At any rate, it was winter in the middle of north central Florida; I was teaching my classes at the university and not fishing. Otherwise I cannot account for my behavior. As if in a dream, I stopped at our library's Judaica collection and introduced myself to the man in charge. "Just offhand," I said, "do you have anything on Jews and fishing? Rivers, water, fish— whatever you can dig up. I don't care what."

The librarian raised his eyebrows as high as they would go, then sighed. "I can see you've never been in here before. Listen, sweetheart, a Jewish fisherman is going to be as hard to dig up as a Jewish athlete. I mean, sure, we all want to be Sandy Koufax." He gave a nervous little laugh. "I'll see what I can do."

Overnight, I considered the librarian's sad eyebrows and felt again that eerie chastisement, as if I'd transgressed and he'd been divinely sent to return me to the fold. Of course I knew the old stereotype. How many Jewish sportsmen can you name, let alone fishermen and hunters of wild beasts? Ask anybody: we've been stuck indoors for centuries, huddled over closely printed texts, difficult theorems, and violins, developing myopia, not to mention serious allergies to grass and trees. The trouble is built right into our linguistic heritage: our scholars tell us that in Yiddish, so famous for its juicy expressions and lively rhythms, there are only two words for flowers—rose and violet—and no names at all for wild birds. To this information, a friend of mine once added, "True, maybe, but we've got thirteen ways to call somebody a schmuck."

It's been said that this linguistic leaning came out of necessity. Our forefathers lived in cramped ghettos inside hostile cities—who had time to go naming birds when any minute the peasants coming down Market Street might turn out to be real evildoers?

But Isaac Kloomok, a scholar writing about the Jewish painter Marc Chagall, exclaims, not without a certain proud petulance, "The Jewish Genius has no respect for nature." He says our struggle didn't start in the ghetto, but goes way back. The ancient Jewish poets themselves are responsible; they showed a deep, even intimate knowledge of the natural world, which they saw ultimately as a "house that has a lord and master." When Jehovah "turns his face away, the shining beauty of the world vanishes. He takes his breath away, and all is dead and withered." So, from the beginning, nature is a pale business next to the luminous personality of God.

This particular scholar was trying to explain how rough it is to be a Jewish painter. "The Jew gave out his expression in song," he says. "He did not create a plastic art." But our writers haven't fared any better with nature. Isaac Babel, a Russian Jew who grew up around the turn of the century in Odessa's Moldavanka Quarter, proclaimed this ignorance of nature "a Jewish handicap to be overcome." In his short story "Awakening" a young boy is forced by his father into violin lessons even though he hasn't the slightest speck of talent. In this family's worried world, the hopes of the whole community rest upon the shoulders of musical prodigies, "those wizened creatures with their swollen blue hands." The boy does the unthinkable: he plays hooky from his lessons and goes daily to the harbor, desperate to learn to swim. But, he says, "the hydrophobia of my ancestors, Spanish rabbis and Frankfurt money-changers, dragged me to the bottom."

He is rescued from this "struggle of rabbis versus Neptune" by a kindly old Gentile naturalist who says, "What do you mean the water won't hold you; why shouldn't it?" This wonderful man becomes a kind of writing mentor too. He encourages the boy to learn the names of flowers, trees, and animals: "And you dare to write?" he says. "A man who doesn't live in nature, as a stone does, or an animal, will never in his life write two worthwhile lines."

Babel doesn't give us a happy ending—or any kind of ending at all. He's a Jewish writer after all, still waiting for the Messiah with the rest of us. In the final paragraph, the boy remains trapped in the book of Genesis, crying out to us his desire to learn the names of things:

> Moonlight congealed on bushes unknown to me, on trees that had no name. Some anonymous bird emitted a whistle and was extinguished, perhaps by sleep. What bird was it? What was it called? Does dew fall in the evening? Where is the constellation of the Great Bear? On what side does the sun rise?

Even as he ponders this, he is being dragged deeper into the ghetto, to his grandmother's house, to wait out his father's anger. He is taken there by a frightened aunt who holds him tightly by the arm, lest he try to run away again from "the smell of leeks and Jewish destiny."

Moonlight congealed on bushes unknown to me too, I wanted to cry, from the other end of the century and another continent. I'm afraid I've got the ancestral handicap, the predisposition for the study of schmucks over trout. My fishing friends are patient: they spiel off information about feeding habits, the names of crucial insects and their stages of development, but I just stand there, amazed by the mere sounds of the words, by the knowledge that there is such knowledge, letting the facts themselves run through my brain as through a sieve. Is this why, in college wildlife biology, I went blank during multiple choice? I married a Gentile who valiantly struggled to teach me the names of a few of Adam's creatures. I'd get starling, goldfinch, sparrow, and he'd be proud, the dazzled parent of a limited kid.

So what's my excuse? God knows I can't claim Yiddish as a language in my life—apart from a few phrases, it went out of our family when my Ashkenazi grandmother Jenny Horwitz died. Nor was I sent to the violin master by my father, who was, in fact, more like the young Babel himself, a deep-city Jew with a confused crush on the wilderness. Under my father's tutelage, we car-camped tentatively on the margins of California's mountains and deserts; we cooked on a Coleman stove and ate Van Camp's pork and beans straight from the can. He couldn't teach us the constellations or tell one cactus from another, but he was forever sighing, his eyes moist with pleasure at the spectacle before him. In our family's most celebrated photograph, he is walking into the vast reaches of the Mojave with the *Wall Street Journal* tucked under one arm and a portable toilet seat under the other.

This was only the beginning: my father's lifelong dream was to live in a house overlooking the Pacific. Never mind that the cliff he selected had a fault running beneath it—this in itself was a distinction, the ultimate proof that he'd gotten out of the Chicago ghetto. I can see him standing on the deck of that house with his hands on his hips, Moses and Balboa at once: "Paradise can wait," he'd cry. "This is close enough for me."

Until his mother-in-law, our grandma Jenny Horwitz, left the safety of Indiana and came west herself to keep an eye on us, the Pacific was my father's domain, all messianic pleasure and no threat at all—a fantastic playground, the great reward. He would drag us out onto the deck to watch the sunset. Once or twice a summer, the newspaper would announce that the grunion were running, and he'd wake my brothers and me in the pitch black of two A.M. to stand on the beach with flashlights, waiting for the miracle of the little fish that came in on the tide and stood straight up in the sand to deposit their eggs.

The house itself—did my father buy it because it looked like a boat?—was long and skinny, with rust stains dripping down the windows. He went so far as to call the lower floor "belowdecks." Even the telephone number pleased him, for it was only one number off from that of a deep-sea charter operation in Newport Harbor, with the deliciously dark name of Davy Jones's Locker. It was for him a matter of special pride that fishermen sometimes called our house in the hour before dawn, wanting to know what time the boat left. My mother felt differently. When the phone rang at that hour, he once told me, she turned pale and held her hand to her breast as if the great trumpet had at last been blown.

For years my father's passion reigned supreme among us, reaching its highest expression in the library belowdecks, where, over the shelves of old medical texts and volumes of art history, and in defiance of my mother's good taste, there hung a huge, stuffed marlin he'd caught on his once-in-a-lifetime fishing trip off Mexico. I used to lie in that room with my eyes closed, taking in the musty and fantastic odor of learnedness all around me. When I opened them, there was the marlin, with its long sharp whatchamacallit pointing north toward the harbor, its glass eyes prophetically glazed and indifferent to the jumble of history beneath. Is this, then, the source of my own mismatched passions—the smell of old books forever wedded to the image of a great fish?

I didn't expect to hear from the librarian, but there he was the next morning, whispering his news into the telephone. "You wouldn't believe, Miss," he said. "I've got a whole cart for you! When are you coming in?"

A two-tiered library cart was loaded down with books, and in the books were heaps of warnings, blessings, fish fables, advice, recipes, amulets, and gravestone symbology—the whole megillah. "Look at this," he said, leaning over *The Encyclopedia of Jewish Symbols*, his voice trembling with emotion. "Long ago, our people fished for their livelihood!" He seemed suddenly bruisable, on the verge of research hysteria, and before I knew it my midwinter curiosity about Jews on a riverbank had transformed into a subject for obsessive study: Fish as Jewish Symbol. That's what librarians do to you, isn't it, or maybe it's just Jewish librarians?

Under his watchful eye, I read everything he gave me. What a mess I'd gotten myself into: a crazy stew of Jewish advice and admonition, centuries of wisdom, leaning toward ecstasy but always holding off the outcome, from the beginning a serious double bind of desire and prohibition—be it the catching of a fish or the arrival of the Messiah. First, the good news. From one encyclopedia I learned that "Fish were created on the fifth day, and God blessed them. . . . Fish, man and the Sabbath are thus connected in a threefold blessing. Moreover the Sabbath is said to be an anticipation of the messianic era which will be inaugurated by the eating of the legendary fish Leviathan." From another, I discovered that fish were believed to bring good luck, and in Eastern Europe some boys were called Fishl as a good omen against the evil eye. From commentaries on the fables of Rabbi Nachman, I learned that in Judaism, water is connected with charity and with the Torah itself: "Your charity is like the waves of the sea" (Isaiah). In the beautiful logic of this commentary, it follows that the *tzaddik*, or holy man, who dwells in Torah is—metaphorically speaking—a fish.

I was rising like a fish myself with all this hope when, in *The Encyclopedia of Jewish Symbols*, I got hooked in the mouth. It turns out that not one name of a species of fish has come down to us in Hebrew. The Old Testament, I read, does not mention any particular fish by name. *Dag* and *nun* are the generic terms covering all species, and by the dietary laws fish are divided simply into clean and unclean. And then I read: "Fishing from a river or pond is forbidden on Sabbath and on holidays,"and I blushed to recall my transgression on the Colorado. A dour entry on fish and fishing noted with mysterious brevity that "the fish cult" probably originated in Babylonia, then spread to Syria and other lands, receiving a high symbolic rank in Christianity. In Deuteronomy, the Hebrews are expressly forbidden to worship the fish. By the time we get to Numbers, our ancestors in the desert are deep in the song of wistful complaint: "We remember the fish, which we were wont to eat in Egypt."

You can see how we lost the knack for the lusty, intimate pleasure of the strike. Add a few dietary restrictions, go inland for a few centuries, and you've got a cultural tendency. I was wading into a swamp of divine and folksy terror, with a smidgen of joy dangled on a line to tease me upward, to give me, as it is said, "a foretaste of Paradise." In parable after parable, smart little fish rise up and advise the fisherman to catch them not now but later, when they're nice and fat. "For then there will be a festival in your house," and so on. Jewish philosophy in a nutshell: Worry now; later, much later, we'll party.

Then it happened. Sitting there surrounded by books, oppressed by the faint but tenacious smell of leeks and Jewish destiny, I came upon a little fish fable that concluded with one of my Ashkenazi grandmother's favorite sayings: "Eat," she used to say. "Eat, or be eaten."

With a grandmother like this, who needs the law? Jenny Horwitz's ghost was rising in a sea of texts, laying her dry little fingers on my arm, making sure she got the last word. She was our family terror: a tiny woman who bristled with business sense and insect phobias, who'd grown up in cramped communities first on one side of the Atlantic, then on the other. She died at ninety-four, when I was nearly ten, but not before pouring into my mother's ears a cupful of worry leveled at nature and the condition of dreamy distractedness it was known to inspire in children. She must have sensed from afar our father's gift for temptation. From Indiana came thick, blue envelopes complete with enclosures on earthquake prediction, the fatal sting of the scorpion, the violin spiders and starved coyotes straying down from the coastal hills, the great white sharks that roamed the Pacific. The state of California was reduced in her private geography to a vortex of catastrophe, in which our house stood dead center.

In the library, I was feeling some thinned-out version of Babel's Odessa fever, looking for redemption in a Jewish fish story, since I was beginning to think I'd never get it on the river—but did I say "redemption," that gift that traditionally belongs, along with fishing and river immersions, in the province of Christianity? No chance. I had a sudden and inescapable vision of Jenny standing over me in the kitchen of our beach house, as grave and prophetic as one of Babel's hydrophobic ancestors of the rabbinate.

She had come at last to California to see for herself what trouble we were in. This was diabolical timing, because my father had just pronounced me old enough to go out on the half-day boat. "She'll catch her death," she cried. This was hard on my mother, who'd grown up under Jenny's worried eye in the Midwest and had, from the beginning, uneasy feelings about the house on the fault line, the marlin in the library, and the big blue chaos beyond. My mother was no match for either her husband or her mother, and for the time being, it appeared that my grandmother Jenny—and the rabbis—had triumphed. That summer I was detained in the living room or taken across the street, away from the ocean and "into town" on obscure errands. It worked. By summer's end, I felt the presence of sharks whenever I swam in the surf—surely the great Leviathan himself waited just beyond my toes, his warm bubbles nearer and nearer. Ten minutes and I would gasp my way shoreward. When I emerged, I knew Grandma Jenny was watching me from the window, pale and shrewd. The dangers of drowning or being eaten alive were only half of it: why was I wasting my time when I could be studying or at least getting smart about real life, on land?

My grandmother has been dead thirty years now, and my father for twenty. But my mother still lives in the house on the cliff. She loves it, she says; she can't bring herself to move inland, though she is plagued from morning till night by salt corrosion, the cliffside eroding under her, the trouble in the pipes my father laid at right angles to save expense, the moaning of the great Pacific itself as the tide comes in.

Not to mention the phone calls. They come, as always, at four in the morning, when she is in her deepest sleep. She sits up in bed and puts her hand to her pale, pale breast. What else could it be but bad news? Beyond her window the waves are banging against the foot of the cliff, and the deep voice on the phone says, "This is Davy Jones's Locker, right? How's the fishing?"

"God only knows," she says, and hangs up.

She takes a long time to get back to sleep, her heart is pounding so, but she never turns off the ringer. "What if it's one of you children calling," she says to me, "and something is terribly wrong? What if they're calling about you, that you've finally fallen into one of your big, fast rivers?"

My rivers? A little miracle: she has gone so far as to link me with rivers. A crazy spark of hope, mixed with ancestral fear, rises in me as it must have in my father when, far out in the Sea of Cortez and out of sight of any land, he got that first tug on his line, the sign of the big fish coming at last to meet him, all beautiful iridescence and darkest warning.

"Don't worry, Mom," I say. "I'm really careful." But this is only partly true. A beginner is bound to wade deeper every time, to cast farther out into deeper waters. I think of Isaac Babel and my father, of that passionate yearning to break into a new world, to discover a new language. Of course it's always dangerous, a new vocabulary. It's the language of the mortal wilderness, not the immortal garden. Maybe they're the ones who keep me fishing, waiting for a local miracle, a foretaste of paradise. I'll think of them the next time I step off a riverbank and into that swift and irresistible current, out of my native element or on my way back into it—who can say?

CATFISH AND MERMAIDS

I'm in the kitchen, beating a catfish to death with a heavy Turkish knife—a small scimitar, really—when my three-year-old daughter walks in. There's blood on my hands, blood on the breadboard. "They're tough to kill," a friend had warned, the friend who'd lent the knife. "Very primitive, all muscle," he'd said. The catfish sweeps its tail from side to side, and as my daughter watches, down comes my arm again, with a fierceness that shocks me. I want to stop myself, crouch low, and explain all this sudden violence and blood to Hannah in a mild motherly voice. But no. I keep right on beating the catfish, until she gazes up at me and says plaintively, "Mommy, please don't cut off the tail."

I stand accused. In my haste to kill the fish, I've forgotten about her obsession with *The Little Mermaid*. How could I? She recently renamed herself after the mythical creature. "I'm not Hannah, I'm Ariel," she said soberly one day, as if she were a medium speaking for some being out of another realm: a secret landscape where the figures of dream and experience are magically revised. Every once in a while bubbles drift up from this place to the surface of our daily lives, suggesting a fantastic underwater garden of roses and shipwrecks a parent cannot divine; at bath-time, for instance, she likes to float on her back in the tub, arms rigid at her sides, letting her hair drift like pale sea grass around her face. Her gaze, from the water, is trancelike, and faintly resistant: am I seeing her first formal protest against the established order? With her ears underwater like that, she can't hear a word I say as I stand there holding out a towel, telling her the water is freezing, and bath-time over now, please.

It's from this realm that she regards me now, with that same unfathomable expression, not particularly horrified but something more meditative, as if my beating of the catfish goes against the rules of her underwater universe, all delicate shimmer and suspension, where words and gestures are not yet freighted with consequence but are instead exotic, sensuous life-forms growing under her laws, her sun. I seem to recall a version of this from my own childhood: I liked to lie flat out on my bed at dusk and say the word *world* over and over again until it lost its meaning and became pure sound, a blue marble rolling in my mouth to match the blue of the night.

But sooner or later, the invisible garden, the pure blue marble of sound, wants to be heard and storied, to have its own beginning, middle, and end; I suspect Hannah's mermaid longings are pulling her this way. Lately, as we read books at night, there is a new look of consternation and demand in her expression, a faint shiver of anxiety in her movements. "What's going to happen next?" she asks. And if I soften the story or hesitate at all, a sharp light glints in her eye. "Tell it right," she says, pointing imperiously to the page. "Don't skip the scary part."

The mermaid identification is to be expected, I suppose: the Disney movie has been out for a while, and even our local grocery store is glutted with Ariel and Sebastian paraphernalia. But it isn't just Disney. I've long since replaced the cheap supermarket Golden Book with a lushly illustrated hardcover of *The Fairy Tales of Hans Christian Andersen*, and she's only gotten more entranced by this painful, beautiful story: the way the mermaid saves the prince from drowning at sea, then hides behind a rock on the shore just as an earthly princess—his future bride—discovers him there. Nor does the violence of the mermaid's sacrifice faze her. In exchange for human legs, the mermaid must give the sea-witch her most precious possession, her voice. And in the original version we read, the hideous sea-witch doesn't just take the little mermaid's voice and put it in a cute seashell for later retrieval, à la Disney. "Put your little tongue out," she says, "and I'll cut it out in payment."

You can see why I'm worried, standing here deep in the early tender days of mother-child unity, about to take the knife to the virginal mermaid's tail. The witch herself warns the little mermaid that when she drinks the magic potion and her tail divides and shrinks to what human beings call legs, "it'll hurt, as though sharp swords are slicing through you." The whole procedure sounds suspiciously like the rough business of first sex.

What primeval witch is at work in me? My God, what if my baby goes mute from the trauma, the little mermaid losing her voice in some gambit with the sea-witch, that big-voiced, big-bosomed, eel-haired octopus of a queen?

And what's the rush for the little mermaid, anyway? Why does she want so badly to surface, even when she understands that she'll have to give up her beautiful voice for the earthly prize of love? I guess we all have it, in love and in the making of art, too: this terrible curiosity to see what happens when we raise our shimmery private worlds to the surface, and win, at last, an audience. And isn't it always dangerous and full of complication, this bargain between two worlds, struck for life? From a world of safety and freedom, we are suddenly thrust into the world of performance, dressed in fabulous but ultimately borrowed silks, and sent out to dance—not sing— for the prince and his court. It's nobody's wished-for element, and never will be, exactly. As the witch foretells, it's horribly painful, and nobody else can know: "No dancer will move so elegantly, but every step you take will be as though you are treading on a knife so sharp that it will bring blood."

Standing there in the kitchen lost in metaphor, I'm shocked by my greedy sea-witch behavior—does she really need to see me kill this fish? It wouldn't hurt to remember,

either, the act of catching the fish itself—even the unglam-
orous, bottom-feeding catfish—since it begins with the desire
to contact that watery world lost to us long ago. It's the first
tug on the line, the sudden flash of iridescence that vanishes as
the fish dives below, and the moment of suspense that follows:
you don't know, for an instant, whether you've got the magical creature or not.

But a split second of mystery is a whole ocean for my
daughter. Soon enough it will be reduced to a brilliant blink of
memory, as the long domestic story begins in earnest, with its
progress of trials, its wishes and human failures, its unpredictable ending. Even in the kitchen you can't get away from
the fact that immortal desires always lead to mortal loss.

Surely it's my job as a mother—especially a contemporary
one—to make my daughter's surfacing a gradual one, to give
her plenty of time in the underwater world of young-girl
shimmer before she flips up to the surface, that second coming up from the womb for air, then again later, up further, to
the grown-up fisherwoman's pleasures of catching, gutting,
and eating that which you have caught.

But the catfish is still suffering on the breadboard, and I'm
running out of time. So I go for the temporary compromise. I
promise to save the tail and cook the catfish whole, if she'll
leave the kitchen now so I can, you know, *hurry up and finish
the job*.

"All right," she says, warily pleased, still innocent. The
mermaid is safe—for now.

"Go play," I tell her, and she exits the kitchen, stage left. Little does she know that I'm about to kill that catfish, cut off its head and fry it neck-to-tail, and that in less than half an hour she herself will eat of it with great grown-up gusto, sea-witch and mermaid all in one.

PART

3

ON LEAVING FLORIDA

As the immense dew of Florida
Brings forth
The big-finned palm
And green vine angering for life,

As the immense dew of Florida
Brings forth hymn and hymn
From the beholder,
Beholding all these green sides
And gold sides of green sides,

And blessed mornings,
Meet for the eye of the young alligator,
And lightning colors
So, in me, come flinging
Forms, flames, and the flakes of flames.

—Wallace Stevens
("Nomad Exquisite," from *Harmonium*, 1923)

Caution to Tourists: Do not enter bushes at sides of high-way in rural districts; snakes and redbugs usually infest such places. Do not eat tung nuts; they are poisonous. Do not eat green pecans; in the immature stages the skins have a white film containing arsenic.

—*Florida: A Guide to the Southernmost State*
(Federal Writers' Project, 1939)

In early June, Newnans Lake is a glossy mud-green, the color of secrets. I take another step deeper in and cast my dry fly, a No. 12 Yellow Humpy made in Montana, toward a faint dimpling twenty feet out, though any rise around here is as likely to be an alligator as a fish. They say there are a couple thousand gators in this lake, and as I cast, one of them groans hoarsely for love in the mangroves behind me. My fishing companion, a colleague from the nearby University of Florida who takes pleasure in testing an outsider's mettle—especially a *girl's*—explains that two big people standing in the water will send any self-respecting gator the other way. But I'm not big, and not convinced. Only my torso is currently above water; choice bits are below, and my companion chooses this moment to realize *all of a sudden* that he's left his grass shrimp on the tailgate of his truck. He thrashes off through the water toward the mangroves, and that, as the nursery rhyme goes, "leaves only one."

I'm beginning to doubt the wisdom of my quest to gain Florida *machisma*, but after six years here, my husband and I will be moving to the West, and this looks like my last chance to get a glimpse of the real Florida. Ever since we decided to move to Oregon, I've felt twinges of anticipatory regret, a disturbing mix of relief and shame over my failure to acclimatize. So when my colleague, a native Floridian, agreed to take me fishing one last time, it seemed like a requisite ceremony, the divestiture of a failed initiate.

In fact, the conditions he set bore all the marks of a ceremonial dressing-down. "Take off those damn hip waders," he said. "And that fishing vest, too—we'll have none of that fancy shit." And so on: I would have to wade in my shorts. I could tote my fly rod and a couple of flies if I must, but I'd better be prepared to put grass shrimp on the end of my tippet if I really wanted to catch fish. I submitted, and now here I stand, perfectly alone, my legs numb, as if they've been anesthetized prior to amputation. Still, this guy seems to know the region's secret places, its guarded heart, lushly complex and easily maddened; like it or not, he's my last-minute guide to a paradise faintly familiar, and more than faintly inimical.

The familiar is simply this: at first, the city of Gainesville, in the north-central region of the state, reminded me of my hometown in southern California, a place I hadn't lived—or known I had missed—for over fifteen years. Even the weekend of the job interview, I felt keenly a sense that any minute

I might round a corner and happen onto a street I knew. Maybe it was the stately palms and sheltering live oaks of the historic Thomas Hotel, with its red-tiled roof and fountains and borders of azaleas, or the orange groves and horse pastures outside the city limits, which reminded me dimly of pictures I'd seen of the San Gabriel valley before development, with its great ranchos and groves of orange trees. But my nostalgia was rimmed with suspense, for here there were coral snakes and alligators, sticky vines curling under window frames, and cockroaches the size of baby mice. In the rainy season, chairs and books were lightly veiled in green. Even the produce was exotic to me: okra, in particular, shocked me a little with its velvety fuzz, its fantastic pearls and slime within. Here was the sensuality of the deeply native—inviting, then rejecting, the stranger.

My husband and I were living in Boston at the time, and apart from the fact that it was winter and our teaching jobs were temporary, I believe I applied for the Florida position out of an obscure mixture of homesickness and curiosity. I went to the campus interview blindly, cheerfully, without even consulting a map, the way you might go to a movie without seeing the preview. All I had to go on was a brief burst of enthusiasm from the university's creative-writing program director (himself a Yankee) when he telephoned to arrange the visit.

"We've got great bird life," he cried. "And you don't need a sweater."

So the seduction began. When I stepped off the plane in Gainesville, it was mid-January and seventy degrees, the air itself some rare form of bliss. The director ushered me swiftly into his ancient sage-gray Pontiac, the color of Spanish moss, and announced that we were going straight to "the Devil's Millhopper." I thought he was making a joke about the interview process, but no, he was in fact referring to a natural phenomenon—a 120-foot-deep sinkhole where the limestone substrata had caved in. As I stepped carefully down the dappled trail in my interview shoes, I couldn't fight the pleasurable incongruity of those fancy black pumps moving down and down into a green funnel of magnolias, dogwoods, violets, and ferns, with little springs running out of its steep sides to form a small pool below. As we stood at the bottom, remote from sunlight, an iridescent blue lizard hesitated, oracular, on my shoe.

That night, after the interview, I called my husband and told him what I'd seen that day: a huge flock of sandhill cranes; egrets and ibises and great blue herons; a big shimmery blue-black bird called the anhinga, perched on a cypress stump with its wings spread wide to dry. Alligators, armadillos, little country stores, and huge trees right in town. "It smells good here," I said. "And you don't need a sweater."

And he: "If they offer, take it."

Back in Boston, we prepared for our new life as if we were going on an exotic adventure-vacation, buying new cameras, maps and guidebooks, and flimsy tropical-theme shirts. We were, I see now, simply an updated version of the naive American settler, the kind who not all that long before us headed into the unknown with parakeet and piano and joyous misconception, only to pitch the whole lot out the back of the wagon months later.

But not yet: even as the close heat of our first summer descended, the seductive nostalgia I'd felt on my first visit held me fast. The birdsong of my California childhood pierced the neighborhood quiet at dawn and dusk: raucous jays, the manic repertoire of mockingbirds, the cool triplicate sighs of mourning doves. The Spanish had come to the west coast of North America as they'd come here, in search of fabled golden cities and unfathomable wealth, and who could blame them? It seemed appropriate, and a little spooky, that Ponce de León named Florida before he actually landed. "Isle of Flowers," he apparently said as he sighted land from the deck of his fragile caravel in 1513. Back home in Spain, they were celebrating the Feast of Flowers, and he believed the place to be an island, so ultimately the name is built entirely out of wish, mistake, and the memory of home—for what else do we have at times of discovery? Once landed, how shocked he must have been by the mysteries of the actual.

Four centuries later, John Muir would register that shock in *A Thousand-Mile Walk to the Gulf.*

In visiting Florida in dreams, of either day or night, I always came suddenly on a close forest of trees, every one in flower, and bent down and entangled to network

by luxuriant, bright-blooming vines, and over all a
flood of bright sunlight. But such was not the gate by
which I entered the promised land. Salt marshes, be-
longing more to the sea than to the land; with groves
here and there, green and unflowered, sunk to the
shoulders in sedges and rushes; with trees farther
back, ill defined in their boundary, and instead of rising in hilly waves and swellings, stretching inland in
low water-like levels. . . . Everything in earth and sky
had an impression of strangeness; not a mark of
friendly recognition, not a breath, not a spirit whisper
of sympathy came from anything about me, and of
course I was lonely.

Although Gainesville has something about it of Muir's
dreamed-of Florida, there is, even so, the hint of a wilderness
without sympathy for the stranger. A kind of magnificent,
aloof patience is sounded by the cicadas at dusk, by the still-
ness in the big pines and sweet gums and oaks, suggesting a
world under the world we've built, just waiting for us to quit
our furious toiling. One old Florida guidebook suggests that if
mankind's efforts to improve the landscape "were relaxed for
a generation, much of Florida would become primeval terri-
tory again." This impression is heightened when you consider
that the state is underlain by limestone, so deeply fissured and
scored with subterranean caverns and passageways that whole
lakes disappear every now and again, like dreams that go under just before we can grasp them.

CO

My rush to connect this new place with my childhood home
turned out to be rather like the last fruit of Eden: irresistible,
a bad idea, and the necessary beginning of my education. I was
informed by my new friends that the cabbage palms and saw
palmettos of north-central Florida had nothing whatever to do
with the tall, skinny "ornamentals" of my childhood—and
that, in fact, all California palms but one were sham, imported
from Mexico and Hawaii and further climes, their leaves
bound in heavy ropes for the trip.

I soon saw the humbling truth of this, how here in Florida
these trees really belong. There are at least thirteen native
varieties, among them the squat saw palmetto of the scrub,
unlike any palm I'd ever seen, with its yellowish leaves and
recumbent trunk creeping close to the sandy soil, sending
down new roots along the way, which in turn branch off and
become new plants. There are, of course, the more familiar
upright palms: the cabbage and the royal, the sable, the co-
conut, and the rare silver. In 1773 botanist William Bartram,
in his *Travels*, was awed by them. You can hear in his breathless
accounts the effort to corral the utterly new into the frame of
the barely known.

> The Palm trees here seem to be of a different species
> from the Cabbage tree; their strait trunks are sixty,
> eighty or ninety feet high, with a beautiful taper of a
> bright ash colour, until within six or seven feet of the
> top, where it is a fine green colour, crowned with an

orb of rich green plumed leaves: I have measured the
stem of these plumes fifteen feet in length, besides the
plume, which is nearly of the same length.

But for me it was the saw palmetto with its strange horizontal
trunk that defeated all expectation and gave me, too, the first
hint of my own doomed-import status. Early that first fall, my
dreams got nervous, as if my psyche were trying to adjust—
or warn me that it couldn't. In those early dreams, snakes
dropped bright and sudden out of trees; a huge gator ran fast
and low across a broad grassy tract, zigzagging behind me
while I went into dream paralysis.

I wasn't far from the truth. If I'd read Bartram first, I'd
have known it, for in between his rhapsodic descriptions of the
flora are passages partaking more of nightmare. In one
episode, the poor man gets in his canoe to catch some trout
for supper and is immediately engaged in mortal combat with
a flotilla of alligators, fending off one after another, each bigger than the one before. "As I passed by Battle lagoon, I began
to tremble and keep a good look out; when suddenly a huge
alligator rushed out of the reeds, and with a tremendous roar
came up, and darted as swift as an arrow under my boat,
emerging upright on my lea quarter, with open jaws, and
belching water and smoke that fell upon me like a rain in a
hurricane. I laid soundly about his head with my club, and
beat him off . . . but could not forbear looking now and then
behind me, and presently perceived one of them coming up
again."

And so on. He manages, finally, to catch and cook his supper, though by then he had "but little relish for my victuals; for constantly watching at night against the attacks of alligators, stinging of musquitoes and sultry heats of the day; together, with the fatigues of working my bark, had almost deprived me of every desire but that of ending my troubles as speedily as possible."

But my husband and I were still newcomers, and Bartram or not, we were determined to continue our love of the great outdoors. Someone urged us to buy a canoe: this, they claimed, was the best way to explore the wilderness. This statement is not untrue. It's just more precise to say that the canoe gives Florida a chance to explore *you*. On our first trip down the Suwannee River, I recall, we were leaning back in the silky air, taking in the hypnotic buzz of insects and the still lifes of turtles on logs, and saying to each other, *I'll bet this is what Eden was like*—when that primitive fish, the alligator gar, with its long snout and studded spine, leaped up into the air and slapped itself down in our boat like a curse. It took us about twenty minutes to get it out of the canoe, with Sisyphean hoists of the paddle, until at last we tumbled it, thrashing, over the side. Our nerves were shot, but the day wasn't over: a few minutes later I went off into the woods to pee and discovered, at my feet, a cottonmouth moccasin—dead, as it turned out, but who can escape one's first impression?

We must have stayed home for a while after that, because the next thing I remember, we had a baby daughter and our cat had taken to sleeping in the canoe. But the wilderness kept calling, as much in the manner of a challenge as a seduction, and when Hannah was a few months old we ventured out again, this time more cautiously. We put her up high in a baby backpack as we hiked the trails of Payne's Prairie, a wetland just south of town—a preserve full of birds, reptiles, and animals, and shadowed by a dark and brutal history of loss. For it was here, in the early 1800s, that the Seminole chief King Payne fell to a band of army volunteers, and not long after that, the long, bloody Seminole Wars began. It was not far from here that the charismatic young warrior Osceola refused to sign the 1833 treaty forcing the Seminoles' emigration to Oklahoma. At Payne's Landing, it is said, Osceola drove his dagger through the table set out for the signing and cried, "*This* is the only treaty I will ever sign with the whites."

Skirting the edges of the prairie and history, we never strayed from the narrow sand trails that wound sometimes through open marsh, other times under dense, darkening canopies of oak trees. When curious friends and relatives came south to visit, however, we found ourselves impersonating knowledgeable guides. We always took them first to the Alachua Sink, a great limestone depression in Payne's Prairie, where dozens of alligators rest nose to tail along the banks of lagoons and waterways. We felt the beginnings of proprietary ease as our friends stepped gingerly along the trails, reported leg-hair pricklings, offered clever if timid similes such as "They look like old ladies' handbags," and "They look like sullen logs." "Thanks for taking us there," they always said afterward, but they looked relieved as they left for the airport.

One spring a famous nature writer came down to visit, and the morning after her lecture a group of students and teachers took her out to Orange Lake, several miles south of town. It was, as I recall, a ghostly gray April morning full of a diffused, milky light touching the hanks of Spanish moss hanging from the great live oaks. Months later, one of the party happened upon an essay of hers that included, briefly, the Florida trip: in her rendering, the fringes of palm leaves swayed against a red sky, the lake was golden, and ticks rained down into her shirt.

Those who'd been with her that day succumbed to a brief, proud spasm of fury, for tick season would not have begun for another month yet, and the mystery of that morning, with its haunting silver threads of light, had gone unexpressed once more. But despite our indignation, we knew ourselves to be as foreign as any visitor lured by the sensational possibilities of Florida, the *what if* of any place where you can't seem to settle down. I could see why she'd surrendered to a red sky, a golden lake, a rain of ticks. It could have been.

As for us, whenever we canoed on a spring creek with our daughter, we held her tight against our own desire to leap into that water, so limpid and full of light, a dazzling turquoise wherever the springs bubbled up through the limestone. A simple, perfectly safe outing, you'd think, if it weren't for the

little white signs posted at intervals: BEWARE! ALLIGATORS.
BEWARE! RABID OTTERS.

Still, we saw great blue herons lifting heavily out of reeds,
the sudden launch and twist of a red mullet three feet into the
air, the long spring creek runs with their water hyacinths and
freshwater grasses rippling out under the surface—a Monet
run amok. For a while we lived in the town of Micanopy,
eleven miles south of Gainesville, a village of rutted sandy
roads and persimmons hanging low enough to pluck without
stretching at all. Our neighbor George, a rangy and generous
woodworker, kept his studio's back door open so anybody
could wander on up any time. His tables and lamp stands were
curved and sinuous, not unlike the snakes he said were "on the
move" in the spring, looking for mates. He warned us pleas-
antly to stay alert: one of them might, at any moment, drop
right out of a tree. It was George who told us the history of
the place: how it had been inhabited longer than anyone knew,
starting with the Timucuans, a sun-worshiping people here
long before the Spanish conquest. The town itself was named
for the Seminole chief Micanope, who refused, along with
Osceola and four other chiefs, to sign the treaty of Payne's
Landing. Osceola himself had once made a bold attack on the
fort here. George told us, also, about the two gods of the
Florida Seminoles: Ishtoholo, the Great Spirit, and Yo-He-
Wah, the one who commands devils and brings catastrophe—
and whose name cannot be spoken in daily life, only chanted

during ceremonies at which he is appeased with dances and sacrifices.

"Have you noticed yet?" George asked. "You dream pretty strange when you sleep on so many Indian graves."

Driving back and forth between Gainesville and Micanopy, on old Highway 44, which cuts across Payne's Prairie, I once saw a sunset that made me think of that split Seminole spirit. It was a sky that only Florida can produce: half of it a row of delicate shell-pink wisps, the other half all fire and flame, like the first technicolor documentary of a volcano. Two skies in one place, like the two sides of a human face in an old tintype, where one half is full of benign light and the other is brooding and sinister.

Maybe it was inevitable. Within a year or two it was the violent sky that we began to see, a god grown too big in our minds. We had no rituals and nothing to sacrifice—only the futile modern lyric of complaint. On our explorations out of town, we awoke to more ugliness than beauty: the paper mills and huge tracts of quick-growing slash pines; the long, high fences surrounding the corrections facilities outside of town. Someone told us there were seventeen such institutions within a thirty-two-mile radius of Gainesville, and we repeated this statistic to ourselves with grim satisfaction. One year, a serial murderer made his nightly camp in the woods just outside of town, coming in to take the lives of five university students in shockingly theatrical displays. The Florida forest, filled with beauty and danger for Bartram and haunting loneliness for Muir, took on another atmosphere in our imaginations. It was a place to fear, a place that drew in solitary nature lovers who never came back—for reasons having nothing to do with wilderness.

With all of this came the strange glamorizing by outsiders. After the serial murders another well-known writer appeared in Gainesville, this one to "commiserate with the community" over the loss of its students. And again it turned out there was another motive beyond witness, only clear to us the following year, when we saw full-page newspaper ads for a novel set in north-central Florida about a series of grisly murders. In the ad, huge oaks loomed over the landscape, their veils of Spanish moss suddenly a symbol of malevolence.

Then, one morning, while my husband was out photographing birds on Payne's Prairie, a man broke into our house in broad daylight; I remember hiding upstairs with the baby, phoning the police and feeling absurdly dramatic, as if I were in a Hitchcock film. The intruder was only a burglar, wanting what he could get quickly, but the moment had its effect. The dangers, not the pleasures and beauties, amplified in our minds. We decided to go west to the Rockies for the summer, joking to our Gainesville friends that it was cheaper to rent a cabin in Colorado than install air-conditioning in our house. I don't think I imagined the slightly questioning look, wise and a little hurt, that one friend gave me, and the way I felt then: that peculiar shame as if, quite literally, I couldn't take the heat.

And, of course, by missing that summer and those follow-ing, with their languorous afternoon parties and ravishing thunderstorms, we never took root in the landscape or the community. Each fall when we returned, the people who'd stayed seemed more deeply attached to one another. I recall the awkwardness at a September barbecue: there had been camping adventures and local jokes; whole worlds had evolved while we were gone. Even our daughter, as she began to talk, seemed not of this place. The sun was a scary god—too bright, she cried—and the big thunderstorms shook her afternoon dreams. So when a university teaching job in western Oregon was advertised, my husband and I looked at each other mean-ingfully. Maybe it wasn't a crime to leave.

There is, in the air over Newnans Lake this June day, the faint hush of a test being administered. I glance over my shoulder toward the mangroves to see if my colleague is ever coming back, and as I do, something long and silver vaults into the air like a knife thrown by a performing chef. Alliga-tor gar, I'm pretty sure, but at the moment it hardly matters. I'm tingling all over, glad to be alive in this place that never stops surprising.

At last my companion emerges from the woods and joins me in the water. He looks a trifle disappointed that I'm still in one piece. We try the grass shrimp for an hour, but there's no action.

"It's not going to happen today—not here," he says in a way that chills me. "Let's get out of here."

It's his property we retreat to, where he has a little sink-hole of his own, a pond he's stocked with bream and catfish and a couple of snapping turtles—along with a big old mud-fish he swears got in there all by itself.

Watching me cast my Yellow Humpy, he sighs. I've got too much slack in my line and I don't know how to set the hook, but I catch bream after bream. "I can see you have the luck," he says, master of the derogatory compliment. "Let me see that thing." He takes the fly rod, lifts it high, and slams the Humpy down on the water, laying the line out perfectly straight, the fly perfectly placed at the edge of the duckweed. Then he yanks it back up so hard the water appears to boil, a tempest in a sinkhole. No fish.

I take the rod back and continue to offer my hesitant be-ginner's casts—the equivalent of the lob in tennis, all height and no distance. This doesn't seem to matter to the catfish that comes blasting up from God knows where to take the fly.

The Humpy, when at last I get it unclamped from the jaws of the catfish, has been neatly disemboweled, the hackle dan-gling from the hook by a slender, intestinelike thread. The bedraggled artificial fly is the victim here, not the fish, like the answer to some question I dare not ask. Yo-He-Wah.

As I leave my colleague's house, I hand him the ruined Humpy. "Thanks," I say. "I'm going."

"Good-bye," he replies. "Good luck out there." He tosses the fly up onto his fish-gutting board, where it instantly disappears among the guts and gills, in the way of all misbegotten sacrifices.

I wave a shaky good-bye and head for my car, keeping an eye on the sandy trail for the cottonmouth, the bejeweled and deadly coral snake. It's June, after all, and the snakes are once again on the move. There's a symphony of smells in the air: harmony and cacophony, everything at once. I can't describe it.

Could I, if I'd lasted longer? Years from now, out in Oregon, I'll still be trying to compose the scent: the nose-prickling fust of marsh, the dank rich of forest floor and the clean sharp lift of pine, the sweet weight of magnolia. I'll swear I smell the delicate orange, though I might be dreaming of that other grove I lost. There's no separating the smells of our remembered places, their skies, their dreams benign and sinister. This Florida, the Florida I'm leaving, won't leave me. It is the lush green vine of memory that grows in my nomad sleep, finding a way into the next wilderness I hope to call home.

THE NIGHT GARDENER

The house came with a garden. This seemed simple enough, until the woman selling the house looked me dead in the eye and said, "We put a lot of work into that garden; it's going to be hard to leave." The woman was an artist, it turned out, a painter. Her name was Drusilla: she had wild hair and the unnaturally steady gaze of a hypnotist at work. Faintly I heard the warning in her voice, the implicit command: you will maintain it, you will not let it die. I nodded, offering what I could to win her favor. We were, after all, newcomers to Oregon, and newly fled from north-central Florida's steamy grip. It would be nice to start out on the right foot. Every climate has its unspoken codes, and who knew what dark laws guarded this lush valley with its benign blue summers, where all those people in covered wagons were headed a hundred years ago, suffering hunger and heatstroke to get to the promised land. This was not a legacy I wanted to mess with.

The rest of the morning was my reward. Drusilla invited me to sit at her table as sunlight poured in. She gave our young daughter a bowl of yellow plums and took me around to see her work. Her paintings tended toward the mystical, the feminine: the sacred site at Delphi, the deep insides of orchids. In another age, she would have been secretly consulted for the healing properties of plants, then burned at the stake. There were wind chimes and strange coincidences. It turned out we knew people in common halfway around the world. "We want the house," I said, forgetting that my husband, somewhere in the house with her husband, might have an opinion about this too.

All summer, waiting for the loan to close, we took friends to visit the house and its garden. She encouraged us to do this. Come any time, she said, and please, if we're not home, take what you want from the garden. Feel free to come inside, too, she said, showing me where they kept the extra key under a flowerpot. The temptation was too great. Once when they were out of town, the three of us ran through the whole house, right up into their bedroom, running our fingertips along the walls. Back in the garden and only slightly calmer, I cut flowers while my husband and our daughter gathered plums, nasturtiums, tomatoes, until everybody's arms were full. Just as we were leaving, Drusilla and her husband came home, catching us on the back steps with our stolen bounty. "Hi," I said. "Is this okay?" Though she was nodding, I felt it again, for the quickest slip of a moment, the dark umbilical between herself and her garden, the way I seemed to have come between them like an invader.

"I've never gardened," I confessed.

She smiled—barely—and held me for a moment with her eyes. Clearly she already knew this about me: this, and possibly more.

"If you ever need help, don't hesitate to call," she said. "We're only moving a mile out of town. If you want to know where we planted anything, say, the delphiniums, please, please call. I loved this garden." I noticed the past tense. Surely this was a sign that she would eventually let go, that I wouldn't be cursed for life. I was spooked, nonetheless.

For the sake of domestic harmony, my husband and I decided to split the gardening responsibilities: he agreed to take on the backyard, with its raised beds for vegetables and perennials, the three-bin composting system, the small lawn. Already he was appraising the beds with a surgeon's cool gaze. "Triage," he said. "We only need about half of it. Our girl's going to need more grass, for cartwheels." Briefly, I admired his fearlessness, his no-nonsense approach, before plunging into my own private sense of inadequacy. For my mission would be to keep from destroying the English-style cottage garden that faced the street, a garden that turned out to be semifamous in the neighborhood. People from two blocks away dropped by to welcome us, or warn us—which was it? "Oh, you've got

Drusilla's garden now," they said. "It's a big favorite around here." Another neighbor was more direct. "I give you a year, two at the outside, before you put in a lawn. Good luck."

But luck was exactly the way it felt, that first season. February: the crocuses came up, small, tentative, easily weighed down, but at last the tulips and daffodils emerged with sturdy authority—even the late-winter rains of western Oregon could not bend them. March, April: a raucous display of azaleas, candytuft, and rhododendrons; a lilac that leaned too close to the driveway, repeatedly wounded by the car. Then it was May, and there were impossible floods of light, and with them yellow coreopsis with blood-red centers, blueberries, daylilies, and a purple butterfly bush already rising above the front window. In July, spires of white phlox shone madly in the moonlight, Shasta daisies leaned heavily against the delicate crowns of Coronation Gold yarrow. I spent hours poring over my *Sunset Western Garden Book*. It was exhausting just learning the names, and my eyes hurt from the violence of all that light.

I cultivated new friends, two of whom turned out to be veteran gardeners. They humored me, escorted me through mazelike nurseries, and stood in the front garden with me for hours, discussing ways to "fill in the holes."

For this was the great mystery: there were holes. Big ones. Places where, I guessed, Drusilla had dug up certain beloved perennials and taken them with her, knowing what would befall them if she left them behind.

∞

It was January: the time of early dark and serious rains. One night we threw a party—a big one—in which the invited and the uninvited mixed in cheerful chaos. Drusilla herself was among the latter, and though she kept to the the edges of the crowd, I saw her every once in while pick up a vase or a book and turn it carefully in her hands in a way that made me think dimly of amulets and little dolls impaled with pins. Midway through the evening, I saw her chatting with my friend the architect, and wedged myself into a nearby corner.

"So what do you think of the garden?" said my friend.

"I think it looks like hell," said Drusilla, swift and sure.

My friend cast a glance my way and I flushed to the neck with embarrassment and something new—anger. Months later, it would dawn on me with no small terror that my friend may have gotten Drusilla to say this while I was within earshot, quite deliberately to make me mad, to jolt me out of my garden dilettantism and into real obsession. And she had pegged me exactly. Standing there in the corner, humiliated and defiant all at once, I privately declared war. I would show this painter—and everyone else—that I could garden as well as the next person.

My rage persisted. It mellowed only slightly with the constant rains of March, mellowed and shaped itself into a youthful determination, oppositional, competitive, deeply immature, but I didn't care. I was going to have my own garden; I was going to fill in the holes. Behind the candytuft and the fading daffodils, I crouched beside a half dozen young delphiniums and a packet of dahlia tubers, which I'd bought because the picture on the cover showed these to be the tallest of all possible dahlias, and of a weird luscious violent color somewhere between chocolate and blood that suited my current mood. This is where I was, deep in April, when Carla called me over to her garden. She was planting tiger lilies, not in rows this time but randomly, in sweet strange groupings. And although it was the middle of the week, her husband was there too, coming and going with a wheelbarrow full of compost. Carla stood up, smiling, and brushed the dirt off her hands. She reached into her back pocket for an envelope.

"Hey, I've been saving these for you," she said. "Five-foot-tall purple poppies. They used to be in your garden—a neighbor told me. They're what's missing. I've always wondered what she had there between the butterfly bush and the yarrow. The colors just don't quite make sense."

She glanced back toward her husband, who was still shoveling. "Maybe if we both plant them, we'll have some luck," she said.

Suddenly I saw it: the faint flush of exuberance in her face, a tentative happiness. I understood that she was not talking about missing colors, or even poppies, exactly. As I accepted the packet, I felt as if I'd taken on something more: hope, or maybe even a responsibility of some kind—very small, very old, a fragile tendril of hope that has moved between neighboring gardens for longer than anybody knows.

"I'll give it a try," I said. "How do I do it?"

As she explained it, I heard the old mysterious tremor in her voice. Some night in the dark, she said, put the seeds on a wet paper towel, put the paper towel in a small Ziploc bag, and store it for two days in the deepest, darkest drawer of the china cabinet. She told me to do it "just so," as she herself had been instructed by her neighbor on the other side. Otherwise they wouldn't germinate. I went home, and that night did exactly as she bade.

It was three nights later, as I lay in bed, that I realized I'd forgotten all about the seeds. It seemed crazy to garden in the dark, but I couldn't sleep. I got dressed, went downstairs, and took the plastic bag out of the drawer. Soon I found myself kneeling in the front garden, the wet paper towels in my hands splattered with dark seed. White phlox towered over me in the moonlight, the bleeding hearts hung their fragile white lockets down, the daisies gave off an acrid, musty smell, almost fetid—how could I not have noticed before? And though the neighborhood was quiet at last, I remembered the voices of Carla and her husband rising and falling in the dark, all those seasons of hope and difficulty pressing up so close to our own.

But the poppy seeds had germinated, and were waiting: they clung wetly to my palms. I had to rub my hands against the soil to get the seeds to leave me. As I knelt there amidst the crazy abundance of that second season in Drusilla's garden, I knew, finally, how to claim it for my own. I kept my hands in the cool evening soil a moment longer. Some people say that plants can talk, can tell you want they want. Can they listen, too?

It's hard to say what I wanted to ask for, exactly. A good growing season, abundance in both our gardens. For a saving magic to bloom between them. "These are for Carla," I whispered.

And I stayed right there, hunkered down in the dirt a little longer than was strictly necessary. It was hard to leave, and why should I? At last, nobody was watching. Everyone was asleep but my garden and me.

MOTHER'S DAY

It was May, and Oregon. In the yellow light of six A.M., birds sang and mated madly above the Sunday quiet of our town. The clock radio flipped on: a man was reciting an essay about the death of his mother, how lately he got a pang of sadness when he went grocery shopping the week before Mother's Day and realized he no longer needed to remember to buy her a card.

"Hey, that's right, happy Mother's Day," said my husband.

"Thanks," I said. "Can you turn off the radio?"

He did, but the next minute our six-year-old daughter, who'd stayed up too late the night before, was at our bedside, shaking my arm.

"Stay there," she commanded, the skin under her eyes puffy and pale lavender. I noticed, groggily, that she was fully dressed, though on weekdays I had to threaten her with no fun ever again to get her to dress for school. "Don't move," she said. "Daddy and I have a surprise for you. Breakfast in bed. Your favorite."

My favorite? Since when? I had no memory of this. We'd only recently acquired our first bed tray, a luxurious item with collapsing legs—but we hadn't used it yet. I did, however, have a distinct memory of setting the alarm the night before so I could grade a few papers before Hannah woke up—was this why I felt a little tightness in the chest? This sort of panic was, I realized, a problem of the late nineties working mother, something to overcome with a five-minute relaxation exercise. I was too tired. I solemnly vowed to act like a mother on Mother's Day, even if this meant staying in bed as commanded until my back was stiff and my mood, well, worse.

Two hours later I was still in bed, exercising this novel form of maternal patience. It turned out the bagel shop didn't open until eight on Sundays. "I'll make breakfast," my husband had offered, but Hannah was firm about the ceremony, and both of us were helpless in the face of her certainty. This was a special day, as she had learned Friday in kindergarten Circle Time, just before the paper hearts were cut out and decorated with more hearts. Love was the order of the day. Mother must be treated specially.

Lying there, gradually petrifying under the bedsheets, I began to have cynical thoughts about this holiday that is supposed to make mothers feel cherished. I'd heard a rumor that it was invented by the greeting-card industry as a merchandising scheme, to stir things up during that long, bleak stretch between Easter and the Fourth. True or not, it has certainly had that effect. The minute Easter's over, the supermarkets and flower shops are draped in shades of rose and pink; the department-store cosmetic counters offer "bonus" totes artfully stuffed with magenta tissue; the newspaper devotes a two-page spread to restaurants serving Sunday brunch, that grievous arrangement of heavy food under heat lamps. On street corners a lone person sits beneath an umbrella, a white plastic bucket of overpriced roses at her feet and a martyred look in her eye, as if she is not selling flowers but hopelessly ringing the bell for the Salvation Army. My husband, thank God, was past guilt, but there was the minor problem of our daughter, her gaze ever more alert to the possibility of a new ceramic kitten, a silver balloon on a stick, the red-heart wands stabbed into the big flower arrangements looming beside every supermarket checkout stand.

The holiday isn't tough on just the immediate family either. It is clear from the onslaught of gifts arriving in padded mailers the week before Mother's Day that mothers-in-law, sisters-in-law, even distant cousins feel the pressure to celebrate and cherish The Mother. Why else pot holders, Amish-folk-pattern dish towels, garden gargoyles, when everybody knows we are trying, as they say nowadays, "to simplify," as in *get rid of stuff.* Aren't they trying to get rid of stuff too? No, it's something deeper: it's as if the mysterious administrators of Mother's Day have sensed in us all some faintheartedness about being cherished, or being famous for our mothering. Maybe it's the beginning of a secret defection from the Promotion of the Ideal—it is, after all, late in the century. Personally, it makes me want to go to work, just to avoid the guilt of my upcoming failure to reciprocate, let alone write thank-you notes.

Eventually the bagels arrived, along with a wilted rose from the garden, and tea sloshing in the saucer. I thanked my exhausted daughter, kissed her hair, and scarfed down the bagel, perhaps too quickly. The day, finally, could begin. "Can I get up now?" I asked politely.

"Yes," she said. "What are we going to do now?"

The truth is, by the end of this day—a nice day as I recall now, composed of two trips to the park, swimming, gardening, a long-stemmed rose in a vase, and a lovely dinner cooked by my husband—I had to face the consequences of my child's noble attempt to cherish me. She was absolutely wiped out, and in tears over her Green Vegetable, which of course I wanted her to eat, and she did not. She surrendered at last, and then frowned. "Mom," she said. "How come you don't play with me as much as other mothers?"

A little wave of panic washed through me. "Gosh, I thought we played all day," I said, trying to soften the edge I heard creeping into my tone.

"I guess we did," she said, but I could see she wasn't convinced. And she looked worried, too, as if perhaps she saw she'd gone a shred too far. "I really like your dress," she said. "I like your hair, too."

"Hannah," I said, holding her tight. "I promise I'll try to do better."

Evening at last, and she was in bed. I stepped into the back-yard to take in the cerulean blue sky, just for a moment, before getting down to the papers I hadn't graded that morning. Why didn't I have that leisurely feeling I'd seen on the faces of French people in their grape arbors at this hour, in films set in Provence? In the yard behind ours there was a low murmur of voices, the creak of a lawn chair. I strolled casually toward the fence. If I couldn't have the illusion of rest and peace in my own yard, why not get it vicariously? This neighbor, a single mother with a wonderful daughter—in fact, the only young teenager I've met whom I'd love to see mine emulate, a girl who makes daisy chains, holds her cat nicely, has roped a chair into a tree so she can "sit in the trees and read books"—this girl's mother, in her chaise lounge, was complaining bitterly to a friend.

"What do I have to do to get her to behave?" she said. "I'm fed up, I'm telling you—I can't take it anymore. And her father encourages her—"

The screen door slammed.

The mother said, "That's it. I've had it. Go to your room, and I mean now."

I sighed, retreated from the fence, and went back into the house to admire my own daughter sleeping. It's true, that cliché about how sweet they are when they're sleeping. The calm face, the great, smooth eyelids, the deep sensual red mouth, slightly open. I stepped into her room. She was hunched up in a ball at one edge of the bed, shivering, and in the center of the bed the sheets were soaked. Once in a while it happens: too much root beer, total exhaustion, the stress of Mother's Day. My heart was full as I peeled off her damp pajama bottoms, then laid her on a blanket on the floor while I remade the bed. She was still utterly asleep, and at peace, and longer than I remembered, as if she'd grown a little since I had put her to bed and turned out the light. I tried to slow myself down, to savor the cool air coming through the window and witness the crepuscular hour: its strange dense blue, the blue of a medieval madonna's robe, so rich that night it seemed rounded, curving protectively down behind the trees.

By the time I crawled into bed myself, I had the delicious feeling I believe I was supposed to wake up with on Mother's Day—well, not exactly. It was better: full-bodied, with a more complex bouquet, this exquisite and tentative relief of all mothers at twilight, imagining sleep.

"So, how was your Mother's Day, really?" said my husband.

"Nice," I said. "But I'm glad it's over."

The next morning in the supermarket, my favorite clerk greeted me at the checkout stand. Her hair, usually brown, had been dyed a violent, junior-high-school red.

She didn't wait for me to say something about it. "Isn't it awful?" she said. "My daughter wanted to do it. You know, for Mother's Day."

She told me she was going to let a decent interval pass, then dye it back to her natural color. On her face was that expression of pride and fear and exhaustion and love we call motherhood.

"She just wanted the day to be special," she said. "God knows, the last thing I want to do is hurt her feelings."

DISTURBANCE

I t began on a Friday in high spring. Three college girls had just moved into the blue house across the street, and most afternoons they sat on their front stoop or on an old sofa they'd dragged out onto the porch. These goddesses were dark-haired and golden-legged, sometimes laughing, some- times serious, but always dreamy, languorous in a way that stung me a little. For whose husband wouldn't notice them, especially in this season of pale and tangy green with a hint of lilac? Mine did, and to his pleasure and amazement, they no- ticed him too, and one day, laughing from their ruined sofa, they asked him if he could spare rose clippings for their Aus- tralian walking sticks—"Petals, thorny stalks, anything," they said. "We don't know yet what they like best to eat."

Now, although he may have looked old to them, he was in fact a young father and medium-aged husband, so along with the bucket of rose clippings—whole stems of flame and salmon and delicate baby white—he wisely took our little daughter along to see the famous insects. I confess I watched all this from our front window, watched him hand over our rose bucket, then lean with our child over a small wire cage. I was jealous, but a tiny flame of pride burned in its center, for three beautiful girls desired my husband's rose clippings, and he, in turn, had taken our daughter with him. This, I knew, was not only for the child's benefit.

Then it was Saturday night, then dark early Sunday morning, and from deep in our separate dreams we heard together a girl's voice rising straight and sudden into the night. My husband rose up with it. Fumbling with his jeans and belt he said, "Listen, wake up, our girls have gone crazy on us."

Our girls, I thought, and the little sting fluttered once more. "Good-bye, be careful, come back," I said.

"Don't worry," he replied. "Go back to sleep."

It seemed to me he was gone a long time. Waiting, I listened to the girl's voice rise higher and higher, breaking hard into the night. *You pig you pig you pig*, she cried, and no man's voice of the many that sang beneath it could hope to rise as high as hers.

Later, back in our marriage bed, my husband seemed worn out. He told me first of all that the disturbance hadn't happened on our block, nor had it been our girls—of this much he was certain. I felt a strange relief, as if I'd won him back. But the story kept on going. He said he thought it was angel dust that had made her so strong, brought her to stand in the center of Harrison Street in her tiny underpants, screaming at the police and friends, and at the crowd of husbands that gathered and gathered, so many of them that he, confined to the outermost circle, never got to see her expression, only how the six policemen finally strapped her to a stretcher, facedown.

"Angel dust," he said, with an urgency I didn't understand. "Did I ever tell you how I once stood at the edge of a circle like this, and in the middle was a guy wielding an axe? Nobody, no police, nobody, could get near him for hours. It gave him such strength. I can't believe I'd almost forgotten."

He sighed. "Good night," he said.

I put my hand on his arm, but he shook his head sadly, like a dreamer shaken from his dream too soon. "I just wish I could have seen her face," he said.

In the morning, next to the newspaper on our front stoop, we found our rose bucket. It was full of petals, brittle now, and pale. All our beautiful petals had been rejected, the salmon and flame and delicate baby white. How could this be? Don't young girls want rose petals anymore? Across the street the door was shut tight, the porch swept clean, as if they'd moved away in the night.

"Are they gone forever, do you think?" my husband said.

We looked again into the bucket, and this time I considered what they'd wanted, what of ours they'd kept. Only the tough stems of the roses, the thorny stalks, the hard nutritious stuff and necessary camouflage.

And though we shook the petals out and went on about
our lives, there was, all that spring, a drift of lilac on the wind,
a swing of light any time we closed the front door. Something
new was living with us now, coming in and out—what was it?
I wanted to ask my husband if he felt it too, but I never did. I
never did.

RHAPSODY IN GREEN

Nature's first green is gold,
Her hardest hue to hold.
Her early leaf's a flower;
But only so an hour.
Then leaf subsides to leaf.
So Eden sank to grief,
So dawn goes down to day.
Nothing gold can stay.

—Robert Frost

A few years ago, when I was married and living uneasily in Florida, I believed that there was, in a town twelve miles away, a little restaurant with green upholstery—a certain green—that served the best breakfast. This restaurant, which I thought existed at a bend in the road near some rail-road tracks, had that sheerly impossible quality we sometimes ascribe to material things, often to restaurants, sometimes to whole cities we can't seem to get back to. If we could only get there again, we think, our lives would be saved, or a deep, nagging mystery solved at last. Surely you've heard people go on this way, rhapsodically, about an armchair they sat in once when they were twelve, or about the smell of sausage in an English pub on a rainy day in March 1957. Some apparently trivial things appear to contain the sublime, and there's no explaining this to anyone—nor any getting over it. Even Proust wore out his friends, trying.

Still, in my mind's eye was that bend in the road, the railroad tracks, and the breakfast house of my dreams. I drove to the town one day, with a friend who puts up with such eccentricities, and found no restaurant there at all, of course, though I'd gotten the bend in the road right, and the railroad tracks.

"Maybe you dreamed it," she said warily.

"Maybe," I said, trying to tamp down the little fear that's been with me since childhood—a fear that, though I seem to get along okay in the world, I'm secretly mad as a hatter.

Then I moved out to the West. And sure enough, that particular shade of green, though not the restaurant, was everywhere. It is a green somewhere between duck-egg and a Granny Smith apple—only denser, richer, a color never found in nature. Sometimes I'd find it in the mud porch of a turn-of-the-century farmhouse, or on the wall of a new friend's bathroom. It had been there all along, in the paintings of Kandinsky and Chagall, and on the occasional umbrella. It was on a T-shirt I wore until I stained it on the day I ate the best oyster of my life and fell in love when I shouldn't have.

This green is not military, not forest-service. Nor is it the color of small imported Spanish olives or the giant ones stuffed with garlic, though God knows I love olives. Their green has its own pleasures, akin to those of oysters—shiny, subtle, harbingers of the primitive, which is why, the day I fell in love when I shouldn't have, I asked for three in my martini. At the time I wondered why the waiter seemed taken aback; the request seemed perfectly natural, no big deal.

We must get beyond, or away from, olives. My green is the color of old walls in photographs of French country houses, of the floors and even the vats of a tortilla factory in Puerto Vallarta three months before I fell in love when I shouldn't have. It is a color you cannot find in the narrow strips they give away in paint stores, where the delusional come searching, aching, for the shade of green they've been waiting for all their lives. Chalky, dusky, somewhere between mint and the color of 1950s tile in the kitchen of the house my husband and I bought.

The owner of the paint store looked aggrieved, as if I'd asked him if there really was a God. "I can't help you," he said mournfully. "That green doesn't exist except in pictures."

Of course not. It can't be found outside, this green—not exactly, though it wants to be, in a way that haunts the edges of almost knowing. It is not the green of pear-tree leaves nor the green of the rhododendron; not even the green-gray of certain aromatic sages that can make you weep for a smell lost from childhood; not even the triple-dark green of a trout stream under cloud cover. Here again, oysters and olives come to mind—along with that feeling of succumbing to something that laps away at the safe edges of your life, though I refused to fall in love anywhere near that trout stream. I was thirty-six and living in Florida when I fell in love with green, but forty and in another state entirely the day I fell in love when I shouldn't have.

I once asked a psychologist if there is a connection between unmanageable desire and a dream of a green restaurant. She laughed but did not explain her laughter. Is this part of treatment?

Just before I left Florida, I took my friend who puts up with such eccentricities to a tiny inland town under a canopy of oaks and kudzu where a hundred psychics live and work. We had made no appointment, but in the town's general store a bulletin board announced the telephone number of the day's psychic "on call." So it came to pass that a woman named Eunice told me what I already knew: that I was "leaving the state," as she put it, and damn glad to be; that I would not miss it one bit.

Then she went on. She said she saw me with my hands in the dirt, and she didn't mean that metaphorically. "You're going to be a gardener," she said.

"Not possible," I said. "I don't garden, not interested."

"Your work will take a turn toward the metaphysical."

"God forbid," I said. "I don't even know what that means."

"You will be lucky in love," she said. "But it won't look like luck for a long time."

We sat a moment in silence.

"Go," she said. "I see a long journey." And then she laughed, and sent me out into her yard, into dazzling uncertainty.

PART

4

THE BOOK OF CHANGES

When a university teaching job opened up in Oregon, my husband and I joked about consulting the *I Ching*, *The Book of Changes*, to see if I should pursue it. We should have known better than to trifle with ancient wisdom— or at least he should have. He'd tried it once before, as a twenty-year-old in Aspen, Colorado, and when he hadn't been satisfied with the first answer and had consulted the great book again, the answer came from the Mang hexagram: Youthful Inexperience. *If he apply a second or third time, that is troublesome; I shall not instruct the troublesome.*

We were heedless, anyway, or desperate to leave north-central Florida. We'd been leaving places ever since we'd met, always on the lookout for paradise, or some negotiated version of it, since our private visions, admittedly, were not precisely the same. My husband had always dreamed of living deep in the country, with a big vegetable garden and a chicken coop, while

I had a hankering for village life, a town where I could walk to work and know my grocer by name. Every time we debated over our imagined future life, old-world superstition flickered lightly in the back of my mind. Was it an affront to the gods to pursue paradise so directly?

But we'd lasted in and around Gainesville, Florida, for six whole years—a record for both of us. I'd gotten tenure in the English department, and after three rentals we'd finally come to rest in a nice old bungalow in the historic "Duckpond" neighborhood. It wasn't the country by any stretch, but the house had a big yard, our daughter was enrolled in a good preschool, and we had a comfortable circle of friends. Still, we were restless, and our dinnertime conversations often re-volved around the steamy climate, the endless straight rows of pine plantations, the crime rate in Alachua County. The job opportunity was at Oregon State University in the Willamette valley, a region praised in the guidebooks for its brilliant springs and long temperate summers, an exuberance of tulips and wineries, blackberries growing wild along the interstates. Winters, we read, were a little dark, but you could always escape to the Cascades or the Pacific, each only an hour or so away. Who could resist such an invitation? We began to dream of raspberries, arugula, sunflowers, and vineyards. Some kind of American Provence, it sounded, and for once we found our-selves sharing a vision of the future. We couldn't shake the feeling that this was our true and awaited home, the one that would answer to that mysterious, gnawing need.

Then, one evening, in a playful mood, we dug the *I Ching* out of the attic. The book emerged from a coating of dust, pungent with mold varieties from at least four states, an olfactory reminder of our chronic restlessness. I pushed that little superstitious feeling aside again, but there remained around the paperback a faintly offended aura, as if thousands of years, not fifteen, had passed since it was last consulted. I thought, obscurely, of the legendary Golem of Prague—a sort of medieval Jewish Frankenstein created to defend the ghetto population from the local persecutors. Woe betide the rabbi who got the Golem out of storage for any trivial purpose—he was a single-minded monster, and knew only how to wreak havoc. It must always have been a terrifying moment, as the incantation to summon him came to a close and the clay figure began to stir.

My husband read up on the method in the front of the book—he was a little rusty, he said. The ancient Chinese used yarrow sticks in a complicated ritual; centuries later, the method of using bronze coins was common. Nowadays, pennies were a sanctioned substitute for Westerners, so, with only a little trepidation, we fished three out of our pockets and asked the question: *Should we leave Florida?* We threw the coins down six times and added up the values of heads and tails according to the instructions, until we had the six lines of a hexagram.

The answer, as I recall, came from the Ming hexagram. *There is no shame in leaving when the lord of darkness is in his tower.*

We smiled at each other. We'd gotten the answer we wanted, mysterious though it was, and I applied for the position. And when I got it, we laughed and celebrated and said to each other, in the semijoking, nervous way of American children raised on a decoction of Grimms' fairy tales and grass-is-greener fever, *It must be destiny*.

And so it seemed. We arrived in Oregon in high summer, and found ourselves dazzled by western light, by cool nights and fruit trees, by an outdoor market abundant with figs, Early Girl tomatoes, slim purple onions—there was even a kind of melon named Ambrosia. We found a comfortable rental house and immediately set out to find our "real house," that home that had so far eluded us. After nine years of searching (between us we'd lived in over a dozen towns, and twice that many rental homes and apartments), we were skilled at recognizing the signs of domestic paradise. We had help, of course. Our ideal was promoted in the catalogs for gardeners and cooks that flooded the mail slot of our rental house, and in the "home stores" sprouting up everywhere, with their wind chimes and ceramic angels, Monet-inspired garden kits and trout-fly welcome mats. We were ripe for the plucking. We searched the real estate notices for an older two-story cottage with a garden, and a fireplace or woodstove if possible. Our old argument about city versus country still nagged at the back of everything, but we soon realized we couldn't afford to be too picky— housing and land prices were at an all-time high out here in paradise.

So when the House made itself available, we did not resist. It happened on a Sunday, in the serendipitous way I'd always succumbed to. Turning a corner, we glimpsed a tiny hand-printed FOR SALE BY OWNER sign on a telephone pole and, a few feet away, a beautiful gray cottage rampant with flowers. A woman in a kerchief was out front, scrubbing her front stoop, and looked up as if she'd been expecting us. "Welcome," she said, and I was flooded with a strange happiness. The house, only a few blocks from the university and the town center, matched our dreams—or, rather, mine, for I thought I saw a little shadow pass across my husband's face as we approached the woman, his dream of living in the country once again pushed to the side.

Still, he said, it felt like home, and there wasn't much else out there. We wasted no time, in the buying or the moving in, and within a few months we began to fill it with the latest trappings of domestic bliss. We painted our kitchen chairs with blue milk-paint, and washed the walls a warm Provençal yellow. We bought an antique oak dining table, and periodically rearranged the living room furniture, trying to get it right. In the backyard, my husband built a pergola for grapes, and a handsome tiled table. He planted a small vegetable garden, and sunflowers against the north fence. He got a book on garden bench designs and selected a cracked antique blue paint for the little garage window frame, beside which grew a vine of purple *Clematis jackmanii* cultivated by the previous owners. The clematis, I remember, was by midsummer huge, spilling off its trellis—had we pruned it wrong? By July of our third year in that house, the year I fell in love and left our marriage, it would topple over with the weight and tangle of itself.

I left in high summer, as if I were leaving not a man I had sworn to love for life and a marriage we had built together, but the feudal courtyard and castle of the Ming hexagram, a dark government of our mutual devising. This is not the way our life looked to anyone else but me, not in this season or any other. It was a catalog Eden, a garden so fragrant and full of fruit it could only be madness to leave. Wind chimes, wavery light on yellow walls, a little girl—our daughter—on a red swing under a pear tree. And I might as well have been Eve, a woman fallen, and, like her, so stunned by my own rebellious reaching, I submitted without question to my husband's request that I leave the house. There was, in my willingness to go, a knotted complexity of guilt and relief, as if a forest of thorny green was rising behind me, to keep me from coming back. The gates of paradise closed, as they had to, as they do in all our first stories of innocence.

I went fearfully out, under cover of my own personal night—a protective darkness no one could penetrate—and with only what I could carry. I made careful joint-custody arrangements, drafting an agreement that would show I was not abandoning my child but had consented to live in another residence to lessen the strain on all of us. My husband and I agreed to a schedule in which we each had Hannah with us an equal number of days, and I was able to find a comfortable place in a neighborhood full of trees and children. I took from the house only what I considered my own: chiefly the piano I'd brought to the marriage, some framed posters, my books and clothes, my writing desk, a few kitchen things. Inevitably, I left behind things I'd chosen with great personal pleasure and paid for, leaving them the way somebody does when they're told to evacuate before a big storm hits. I told myself I didn't want to denude the house—especially for our daughter, I wanted it not to look too different. I told myself, too, that mere things, the home place itself, did not matter to me. But the night before I left, I lay in bed staring up at the slanted dormer wall. It shone pale gold from a streetlight, veined with the shadows of tree branches; any minute, it might speak out of its abandonment, and make me homesick for life. I had the crazy urge to apologize, the way I had to my husband—a desire no less real for being futile.

It wasn't until late fall that I began to miss the house in earnest, and to realize, in the simplest physical sense, what I'd left behind. My old guitar, from an era long before marriage; a box of eccentric Christmas-tree ornaments given to me by my dearest friend, which I'd stashed away deep in a closet, awaiting the next holiday season. A tall antique cupboard in crazy blue, five layers of paint speaking to its own migration through houses and time, sometimes passed from mother to daughter but, at some point, from a daughter to a stranger, and on to me. Who knew what histories were buried in those layers?

I went back, nervously, tentatively, for certain things: the guitar and, for my daughter's room in the new apartment, the aquarium I'd bought for her the year before, which, my husband told me, had always driven him crazy with its mad burbling. The front garden itself, which I'd tended, presented a problem. He would not, he said, be able to take care of it, and was thinking of putting in a lawn. Who could blame him? It had the signature of my private struggles and pleasures all over it. So with a friend I came one day at a designated time and uprooted the plants that meant the most to me: the dark red twelve-foot-tall dahlia, the irises and delphiniums. We took them to her place "for foster care," as she put it, a phrase that seared, as did the sight of those flowers, their roots in ragged little cloaks of soil, being carted away, evacuated from the scene of impending disaster.

On the days I come to pick up my daughter, I cannot linger, for the haunting hasn't yet begun to fade. This last December, particularly, I remember. The front garden was still intact— perhaps, after all, my husband would not put in a lawn—and memories of our three winters there came back to me whole and sudden: how I'd always wait till the last minute to collect the leaves of the English sycamore and push them into the street for the city truck. These are huge leaves, bigger than a big man's hand, and as I came to the front door on one wet, windy day, they collected accusingly around my feet. They clustered in corners and heavy clumps at the foot of the front steps, a reminder of the gravity of change.

It is late February. Still the wind bangs at the gate and my lost garden is a world as ghost-ridden as a cemetery, where the dead are forever affronted by the terrible dispatch of the living, our insolence in moving on, in forgetting them so fast. But the exile, even the one who decides to leave, is not without longing, not without grief. I am a little afraid of this house and of the spell that seems cast over it. Not Eden now, but the castle in the story of Briar Rose, it appears to have a fantastic thicket of thorns around it that protects the sleepers within from the mortal shock of a sudden rupture, until they are ready to awaken, and carry on.

I have, over the fireplace mantel in the apartment I share with my daughter, a framed poster I bought in Paris, on one of the last trips my husband and I took together, the trip on which I felt the first flutterings of some deeply buried despair, the need that would become, two years later, that strange, unbidden blooming of love and the desire for flight. *Jardins and Potagers Naïfs* reads the script under the painting. The house in the picture could be ours, or the vision of it in which we first

met and held our hands around that fragile flame of a life together—though how to really make it ours may be the place
where we slowly, secretly, diverged.

In the picture it is high summer, and the viewer stands
beyond the little gate, looking at the geometric rows of a
garden and up a central path that leads to a pink cottage with
pale blue shutters, a red roof. The gate is barely open—
barely—and, close to the house and far away from us, sits a
velvety gray cat, disproportionately large, as are the cabbages
and pumpkins of the garden. These are the deceptively simple
pleasures of the naïf, its seductive distortions, its yearning for
the dreamed-of harvest.

There is no gardener in the picture, but a watering can, as
gray as the cat, sits halfway up the path, waiting, it seems, for
the gardener to return. There is, about this picture, a sense of
calm and verging suspense all at once.

Meanwhile, here outside the gate, it is still late winter. In
my old garden the leaves gather and whisper; they pile up near
the front stoop. If they had eyes, they would look on me with
the same raw unease I saw in my husband's eyes that summer,
and in the eyes of so many of our friends, veiling their own
ripped places, hiding the bitter taste of old sorrows awakened
by this act committed so nearby. We can't speed the passing of
the season; it will happen in its own time. Still, I can't help but
wish spring were here for my husband, bringing with it the
desire for new growth, for restoration and first harvest.

But that is his story to tell. I know only mine, and that, only a little. In it, the watering can sits exactly where I left it, in the garden to which there is no returning. I have taken myself out of the frame and beyond the pale. The plentiful summer is far in the distance, but I can see it there, even as the gates close behind me on the aching beauty of the naïf's paradise and I stumble forward, amazed, into the wilderness.

her, and what could I bring there, what healing instrument do I have that is as powerful as a child's wish to go back to the unity she was promised, in the deepest way, by being born to us and brought this far between us? Her own load, our own hearts and guts gone heavy with anger and grief and confusion, she carries. What can I do but try to carry some of it for her; take some of it, offer a "lightening" as physically as I can? So on those nights when she is with me, and I am putting her to bed, I lay my hand on her small warm belly and rub in a circle. "Oh, Mom," she says. "That feels so good. Can you do that every night?"

The swirl of darkness and the desire for the return of unity—of light—will live in her forever now: there will be a mystery there like the mystery of where God went, so long ago, and our waiting for that return. The tug of us, that which created her then broke apart, will be a wish that lives in her like religious faith, her eyes forever trained on the secret story of the world. Maybe, just maybe, it will give her the faith to trust that no mortal's answer will ever be the right and only one.

Each of the blanket's halves is still intact, though she recently told me that the one at Daddy's house has lost most of its stuffing and is, as she put it, pretty wrecked. She looked at me long and hard. Could I come to the house and fix it? I held her hands and composed my answer carefully, knowing now the power of the word. "I can't, sweetie," I said. "I'm sorry." Someday soon, only she will know what that blanket once

SOLOMON'S BLANKET

When my husband and I separated, there arose the problem of where to keep our daughter's beloved "sheep blankie," a blanket already small, already so worn that its stuffing was falling out and the sheep themselves had faded to white. I was the one wanting to leave our marriage and, as such, found myself performing the dark rituals of rupture, tearing, in ways small and large, the fabric we'd woven for twelve years, never checking the seams. I asked a friend to split the blanket in half for me and sew up the open ends. So now there are two sheep blankies where before there was one, each diminished, and their inevitable ruin charged with deeper significance.

"The Solomonic sheep blankie," said my husband, with a sober, warning look, when I handed him his half. He was right, of course, and I knew it. The spiritual cost of leaving was unknowable, and I was beginning to see that it would come out over the seasons, like the unpredictable winter weather of our Northwest valley, a landscape where, in this season, a squall rises up over the coastal mountains, runs its course, and subsides, only to be followed hard upon by the next. It is difficult, even in the best of times, to remember the greening of the valley that begins under the low and rolling tumult of clouds gathering force over the ocean, where we can't see it.

Our daughter herself is the baby of Solomon's challenge, in that story in which two women vie for possession of a newborn and the King calls for a knife to divide the living child in two, "that they may each take a half." So it seems to me, anyway, when I hear Hannah tell her teachers and friends with stunning directness, "Did you know I'm separated?" There is nothing more true: she is divided between us, the separated halves of our influence, our selves carried in herself. She carried us inside her before this, I know, but then the two halves were mingled—who knew where one left off and the other began? Who ever thought about it? This is something we are usually granted to know about our parents long after we are grown, and they are gone.

But Hannah, at six, is doing the heavy work of conveying stories between our houses, carrying our identities themselves. The stories are always beautiful ones, romantic even, and in her voice is wistful pride and a hint of wise admonishment, for the moments of discovery and beauty we each miss by seeing her only half the time. At Daddy's, she tells me, there is a wild mouse. They have never actually seen her, she

says, but this mouse—a girl mouse of course—is there as sure as anything. Hannah has even named her: Wild Blackberry, for this is what the mouse would eat, if she were given the choice. Conversely, I've heard her tell her father on the telephone about my new landlady's ancient cat, nineteen years old, playful and loud voiced, but with a diagnosis of liver damage. Hannah regularly says a prayer for this cat, whose name is Nesta. *Please don't let her die yet.* Nesta's very name calls up the single nest of the ideal childhood; the cat herself is a tough survivor whose death we can only hope will be delayed until it is less painful.

There are darker currents than this. They are harder to detect, more troubling, and I find myself praying that these too will pass like our valley storms, bringing glimpses of light between, and the slow greening beneath. But when she is in one of these moods, it is the very darkness itself. She recently drew a self-portrait of a girl in tears, out of whose mouth comes "ha ha," and arching over, where a year ago a rainbow would have been, are the words "I am nothing." To read this is to be scalded by grief and fear. Yet when I asked her what "nothing" felt like, she gave me the key to helping her: she pointed to a precise spot between her heart and stomach, and said, "I feel it here, when I think of you and Dad when you used to be together."

The place where we were once joined in her is a real landscape between heart and gut—a place I am afraid to journey. And how to go there? What words would carry me inside

really looked like: the sole archaeologist of her own early life, studying the artifacts of a lost country, or a mountain reshaped by rough weather.

She's been asking me, lately, if God made us, then who made God? Nobody knows, I say, and I tell her a story I heard once when I was young, a creation myth from the Zohar, the thirteenth-century book of Jewish mysticism.

One day, I tell her, God was feeling lonely, sort of empty inside, and he sighed his loneliness into the little space of nothing that lived beside him. But the sigh was too much for the space of nothing, and it exploded, like a great big sneeze. Thus was the universe created, a darkness full of burning lights and bits of rock, where life itself would begin, over and over. So it is that everything in the world has a spark of the Divine inside of it—trees, rocks, you name it, I say.

Even me? she asks. I have a spark inside me? Where is it?

What luck a story brings; how often do we get this chance? I put my hand on the place she has shown me, between heart and gut; the place that aches and remembers; that sometimes feels like nothing.

That's where it is, I tell her. Right there.

THE PET WARS

W e'd been separated a month when a friend suggested to my husband that he get a dog. This, our friend said, would not only cheer him up, but make the house highly attractive to our six-year-old daughter, who would be moving between our two dwellings. I heard it from Hannah, one day when I picked her up from school: "Mommy, guess what? Daddy's getting me a golden retriever for Christmas."

But it was only September: Christmas was a long way off. Hannah, arriving at my apartment, regaled me with the details of future bliss at Daddy's: chiefly, the way this dog would pull her along on her Rollerblades. "Wow, neat," I said, inwardly riven by that lowest of human passions: envy. But as dark luck would have it, even in this sonata there were sags—who, at six years of age, can sustain the high, sweet melody of anticipation for longer than a week? How long is it till Christmas? How long is a month, how long is four? Christmas became an apple too high to pick, a foreign country, a comet that never seemed to move across the sky. Then one day she was buoyant again: "Daddy got me an Australian walking stick, until we get the puppy." I smiled my terrible false smile. How come I hadn't thought of that? I was losing ground every day in what felt, obscurely, like a competition to make our baby happy, happier, happiest. But the walking stick died within three days of purchase; then a pet rat, borrowed from a friend for a week, had to go home again.

There were, actually, other, long-term pets in Daddy's house: our old and slightly edgy cat, Squeak, and a small aquarium with two neon tetras and a shy plecostomus who vacuumed algae off the tank walls at night, when nobody was looking. But these were pets associated with me, and not very cuddly besides. It wasn't long before my husband telephoned to say that the aquarium would be waiting for me on the front porch. "Come and get it, right now," he said, in a voice that suggested ultimatums at the state level, the nuclear nerves of nations who've been betrayed and are playing their cards one at a time.

I tried to calm myself; there was no hope of competing. I lived in an apartment within a house, beneath a very kind landlady with two cats of her own and an apologetic but firm stance on the pet question. Still, the stirrings I felt, down in the pit, worried me some. They would out, sooner or later— this was the story of my life. I tried various strategies to make peace with myself. I drove the aquarium back to the apartment

carefully, so it wouldn't slosh over speed bumps, and ensconsed
it in a safe corner of Hannah's room. Then I telephoned a pet
store to ask if I could add a salamander to the current population. No go—three fish for a tank of this size was apparently
the limit. Surely, I thought, something would die soon, and
make room for a new, cute creature Hannah would notice. But
none did. The plecostomus, particularly, had a canny, stubborn
look. I tried telling her stories about the fish, to make them
seem more adorable, and I put a sticker award system on the
wall so she'd be motivated to feed them herself. I encouraged
her to talk to the landlady's ancient cats, treat them like her
own, though the elder cat was ailing, so, said our landlady,
"No more picking her up, please." Very tentatively, I asked my
landlady how she'd feel about a hamster, and the answer was
a reluctant no. She had, very reasonably, images of "pellets"
on the apartment's pale blue carpet.

As the fall deepened, I tried petlike but inanimate things:
a cozy afghan, Halloween pumpkin lights strung along the
mantel, a nightly fire in the woodstove, hot cocoa with marsh-
mallows. But still, the exquisite melody from Daddy's house
poured into the porches of my ears. "Daddy says when we get
the golden retriever . . ." and so on. By now, Hannah's eye
for this beautiful breed of dog was wondrous sharp, and in
fact, suddenly, there were golden retrievers everywhere. We
couldn't take two steps without seeing one: puppies, adoles-
cents, full-grown goldens, the last of these backlit by a beautiful autumn sunset and standing protectively beside his

owner, who in turn stood behind his lawn mower in the ar-
chetypal pose of one of Millet's plowmen: beautiful, noble,
lonely against the mountains and light, while I sped along in
my small and faulty car, back toward the little apartment.

Then, one day, the landlady stopped me as I headed to my
door. "A hamster is okay," she said uncertainly. I nearly em-
braced her. I managed, over the next few weeks, to keep this
news a secret from my daughter, waiting for the right moment
to tell her. But the longer I waited, the more squeamish I got.
One of my friends said darkly, "Don't get a hamster; they
break easily." And another friend, of somewhat feral disposi-
tion when it comes to marital strife, said, "Get it quick, before
he gets the dog." She went so far as to recommend a creature
called a "great golden hamster," so that I had images of a hamster the size of a retriever, its furry silhouette glowing in the
light of my woodstove of a winter's evening, or harnessed for
the pleasure of a Rollerblading child.

At the pet store I admired something called a teddy bear
hamster, which looked like a small piece of shag carpet. And
yes, said the pet-store man, it was a highly breakable pet, but
awfully cute. I nodded, succumbing. I had, in fact, great faith
in my daughter, whose favorite words that fall were *delicate*
and *brittle*. Her touch was so tender she could transport the
most fragile of walking sticks from finger to shirt to jar without breaking off its limbs—God knows she could handle a tiny
hamster. But the pet-store owner began to frown. "On the
other hand," he said, "a hamster's like a water balloon. When

you squeeze 'em, they tend to sort of squirt away out of your hand." I was stunned by this description, but he was already onto another subject. "But a guinea pig, now they're solid. You know you've got something in your hand when you're holding a guinea pig." I agreed to buy a book and study up first.

The book on guinea pigs was sobering. *Are you prepared for longevity? Are you prepared to clean up vomit, urine, and the occasional "other" accident?* The future was more perilous than I'd thought, and I'd already thought it pretty perilous. I was rescued, that very afternoon, by my daughter's announcement that "Daddy and I may not get a retriever—he found out they're very expensive, and a lot of work. But"—and here she brightened—"we might get a little kitten at Christmas." And suddenly, I could envision my husband in his parallel but oh-so-separate universe, standing at other book racks, talking to other pet-store owners, going through the same agonizing realization that I was, that the pet-as-solution was a fantasy.

Then, as if the facts of veterinarian expenses and vacation arrangements weren't enough, Hannah turned out to be allergic—mainly to grass and trees but also, slightly, to cat and dog fur. "The warm fuzzies aren't a good idea for her, I'm afraid," said the doctor. And she, with her breathtaking logic and love of jokes, added, "Mommy—I'm allergic to warm-blooded animals. That must mean I'm allergic to myself."

Time passed. The mythical kitten had faded now, too, and I was taking Hannah once a week to the allergist for shots, while she hung onto the car door handle, the chair arms, the receptionist's counter, and I cajoled and pulled and tried not to look at the other patients watching us in horror. This is one of the mysteries of life: from the desire to get a hurting child a pet to the reality of making her Wednesdays a waking nightmare, in less than two months. It is uncanny, the way life refuses to be a fairy tale.

In the end, Christmas passed uneventfully. No dogs, cats, or other creatures, warm-blooded or cold, were added to the nervous menagerie of our transition. Then, in January, the day before Hannah's birthday, I found myself in the pet shop again, deep in the rodent department, as if I'd gone there under hypnosis. Such a small animal, I thought to myself, and not that much fur, when you come right down to it. Hannah had been allergy-free for two months, even with Squeak still in her life; the shots were working miracles. This was not good medical thinking, I realized dimly, but maybe we could call it a trial run. So it was that without glancing at a book or asking a single question, I took the owner by the sleeve and pointed to a litter of velvety gray rats with black eyes. "I want one of those," I said. "I'll be back in an hour; please set me up with everything I need."

He did. I got the glass tank with the screened roof, the water bottle with the metal tube, the exercise wheel, the pine shavings and mixed nuts, the works. So it was that Tom the Rat entered our lives. An easy pet, he goes where Hannah goes, back and forth between our houses, learning to trust our hands and sleeves and shirt pockets, our collars and hair, even his clear plastic traveling ball. And though I wait and watch, there's been no sign of an allergic reaction from Hannah.

Is there a sigh of relief in the other house? I may never know. But I like to imagine that Tom the Rat keeps us all company in the night equally, with the same little sounds, this nocturnal blessing. Hannah and her daddy, then Hannah and me, but always Hannah, as he makes his small comforting noises in the darkness of a child's night. I hear him now, as his delicate tongue rattles the metal ball of his water bottle. There is a pause, then he steps up onto his wheel again, and slowly, slowly, begins to make it turn.

THE CONTAINED GARDENER

One day in January, a seed catalog arrived in the mail. I was astonished; how had they found me? I'd been lazy about filling out change-of-address forms—lazy or something else. My marriage had broken up the summer before, and the fall had been a long, dark season of letters and phone calls not only from friends but from the circulation managers of magazines, who seemed suddenly prescient: *Have you moved?* I knew this was nothing more than low-grade paranoia, but it felt like cosmic meddling when I wanted nothing more than to disappear. That January day, however, I found myself holding the Shepherd's Garden Seeds catalog with uncertain pleasure, as if it were not simply a seed catalog but a first invitation to live in the world again, to work the soil and plant things, an act, for me, fraught with significance. My old garden itself, with its rampant blooms, its unconscious leanings toward big chaos, seemed now one of the unrecognized seeds of my own unruly growth.

I felt humbled about the desire to garden again. This time, I said to myself, I must do it in the smallest, least ostentatious way, or risk cultivating that native raucousness of character that got me here, to this patio apartment, in the first place.

The catalog, when I began to flip through it, fell open with a natural ease to the pages on container gardening. *A lack of terrestrial garden space need not deprive you of this pleasure. Containers make possible satisfying portable gardens, even in slivers of space on a deck, a balcony, or the front stoop.* I heard in those first lines a patronizing, charitable voice, clearly the voice of someone with lots and lots of garden space, and a spotless record of marital behavior. The voice made me deeply suspicious, then began, as such voices always do, to tempt me in the direction of restlessness, gigantitude.

For those of you wishing to make the best of constrained circumstances, it should have said. *For those of you who have made a mess of your old yards. For those of you trying to keep a low profile and a low overhead, until such time as it is seemly to garden with big flamboyant gestures again.* Forget it. There followed a list of phrases surely calculated to overstimulate an anxious gardener's winter nerves, to haul her, untimely, out of guilty hibernation. Superb Super tomatoes, red and green French mixed lettuces, aromatic petite bushes of Fino Verde Piccolo Basil, red alpine strawberries, *the tiny berries of which have an intense flavor we can only describe as a heavenly combination of strawberries and roses.*

Dukat dill, cilantro, leafy, *slow-bolt type* French chives, fine mild flavor. Not to mention the flowers: Wine Series Salvias and Lilac Regatta. These people were diabolical, and my resistance was down. Did they really want to sell seeds, or just ruin a life with images of a Provençal garden and a bottle of a nice rough red?

Order now, it said. Start early.

I put the catalog away and rebuilt the fire in the woodstove. It was, after all, only January. Wait. If you can't behave appropriately in the eyes of the world, at least be quiet. As the great essayist Montaigne wrote, "The value of the soul consists not in flying high, but in an orderly pace. Its greatness is exercised not in greatness, but in mediocrity."

Could this be applied to gardening?

When I left the house we'd shared together, I took a few plants with me. Maybe if I examined the list, I would understand some important psychological pattern. Blue flax; yellow coreopsis with blood-red centers; a little mound of pinks; and, in a big pot with a wobbly trellis, a New Dawn climbing rose I'd bought only that spring, dreaming of a whole fenceful of the white-going-pink blooms, whole clusters of them, abundant as grapes, the way I'd seen in some Oregon cottage gardens, a crowd of roses, so many of them they seemed suddenly a peasant flower, gregarious and earthy and madly abundant, no aristocrats, not interested in big symbols, just a good time . . .

Making a list is a bad idea. It only leads to fantasies. Luckily, there is another model that fills me with pleasure, with a sense of possibility within the realm of the contained. This is the tiny patio garden of my mother's housekeeper and my beloved Nana, Mrs. Rodriguez. At the back of her house in Alhambra, California, was a little brick patio, surrounded by wrought iron "to keep out the gangs," as she once said, dismissing them all with one wave of her small hand. Into that small square patio, she had brought her memories of a Mazatlán childhood. A big avocado tree stood in one corner, and there were big terra-cotta planters of hot peppers and tomatoes. And flowers. I don't remember precisely what they were; only an impression of heat and light remains: yellow and red and orange. "Take some," she'd say, reaching with her long pole and filling a paper sack with avocados, more than our family could possibly eat before they went bad . . . as well as tomatoes, peppers. "I have too much," she'd cry. "You have to take some, *mi hija*." Everything was in pots, and everything spilled madly over, like her laugh when she plucked dead leaves away and said of one plant, "Oh this one, it gives me so much trouble. But I can't get rid of it, you know what I mean?"

My patio apartment is the lower half of my landlady's house— she raised four children here from the 1950s on. The house sits on a hill. From up here we can see steeples, a beautiful dark-red brick building that must be on the Oregon State University campus, the plume of steam rising from the university power plant, the top of the gymnasium, the dark green heaviness of Douglas fir. There is something of the hidden villa to this place, and though the little rented apartment is officially a basement, the family's old "rumpus room," my landlady and her late husband wisely designed it with big picture windows at one end, beyond which sits a stone patio. Each morning in the dark of this winter I lit a fire and pulled the curtains open; there was no way to do this without feeling both extravagant and subservient, like the curtain boy at the opera, great long pulls, waiting for the audience to gasp at the fantastic set.

At first it would still be dark. There were only lights, and gradually the power plant's white plume held shapely by the cold, and the black dome of stars we are granted, even only a mile out from town. But then came the Oregon winter dawn, an exquisite veil of icy blue, and for a moment I could imagine the white roof of the downhill neighbors to be covered with snow. At last, light stunned the sloping greensward, my landlady's perennial beds and fruit trees, everything still bare, but a known wealth in spring and summer. I nearly cried the first time I saw it—how could I deserve this luck, to leave one garden in shame, only to be granted the gracious, expansive view of another; this one was older, more stately and set out, to be sure, but even that seemed right, part of the humbling, the slow rebuilding, the observance of order and form Montaigne understood.

My landlady had generously offered space in the beds for anything I had, but for now I asked if she'd mind a few containers on the patio. I wanted to garden small, contained, modest. A Montaigne garden, for now.

She hesitated slightly. Perhaps by now she knew me well enough to suspect that something would spill over, that I was not, by nature, patient and aesthetically fine-tuned enough to be a container gardener. But she agreed. Okay, she said. Let's give it a try.

The winter passed, and the rainy spring. It is June now, and the time is right. I didn't buy from the catalog after all, but went, with great ceremony, to the biggest nursery in our county, where I bought twenty plants, two long wooden window boxes, and a big terra-cotta pot. When I'd filled all the planters, I still had ten plants left—clearly I had no sense of just proportion. This, of course, necessitated a second trip to the nursery, during which I could not resist the purchase of another couple of herbs along with my three new pots. By the time I got the balance right, half the patio was edged by planters. It didn't exactly match my vision—a bit too exposed and sad and linear, my little attempt naked to the world—but looking at this bare beginning, I understood suddenly what a container gardener *could* do, *could* be: Mrs. Rodriguez's patio, with its sense of hanging gardens, of secrets and pleasures hidden from the public eye, yet remained in the offing, to be aspired to. My landlady, meanwhile, looked a little concerned, but said nothing. And so the new season begins. I have herbs in one long window box: Thai basil, thyme, and oregano; in the other, I've planted lobelia, a rose from a student of mine, and a deep red pansy chosen by my daughter, whose taste, I suspect, runs to the bright and hot like mine. The New Dawn is blooming now, twenty roses a day, and it looks like it wants out of its pot.

Not yet, not yet. I water like a madwoman, or a new mother. The plants in their little containers are as hungry as infants, and growing over their pot edges in miniature rampantness. I water so thoroughly, and so often, that it begins to feel like a form of prayer. I still dream about the old garden, and whenever I go to the house to pick up my daughter for the week, I see that the garden is more enormous than ever. My gaze roves out, ever casting toward it, and toward all the beautiful chaotic cottage gardens of this town. It is prime gardening season. Everything appears to be blooming all at once, though this cannot be true. I take a few deep breaths and quote Montaigne to myself. It's almost too much for me, the plenitude of the right beginning.

granddaughter and tried to tell me it wasn't true. I only remember thinking that if Jesus on his crucifix saw Nana holding
my hand, he would know I wasn't completely bad.

So it was that I was escorted through a new world that
tugged both ways. For a minute I wanted to run from the dark
mission, back to the safety of my own smooth gray sidewalk.
But there was the great mouth of the church, dark as a cave,
with little lights burning in their red glasses. Something
waited—what was it? Was it this Nana understood? For she
took my hand and led me forward, whispering, "I know I
shouldn't. Your mother wouldn't like it." Then she looked at
me, sighed, and we stepped together into that fantastic new
darkness, lit by stories I didn't know.

When Nana and I meet at her back door today, she cries out
briefly at the flowers, then quickly lets go of her walker and
holds me close. When, after a long minute, she looks at me, it
is with such joy that I am flooded with relief. "Listen, *mi hija,*
don't feel guilty forever. You never know when love is going to
come to you," she says, her eyes bright with tears. "It can happen very late in a life." Slowly, and with great effort, she holds
the screen door open and gestures me in.

We put the flowers in a china pitcher in the dining room,
a burst of unruly color in this small house as clean and still as
a museum. I realize suddenly that when the flowers wither,
she won't be able to throw them out herself; that she'll have

to wait for one of her daughters to come help, on a grocery day. "My granddaughter Linda will take care of them," Nana says, as if she's heard me. She moves toward her armchair, nodding in the direction of the back patio. "I used to have so many plants, remember?"

She sits down in her favorite chair; a broken ottoman tilts awkwardly at her feet. She dismisses it with a wave of her hand. A long sideboard is crowded with pictures of her children, grandchildren, great-grandchildren, and so is the wall above it: the pictures all hang a little crookedly—they always have, from the vibrations of the passing trains. Her walker stands before her armchair. The couch and two other chairs appear brand-new, untouched.

"I almost forgot—I want you to have something," she says, and starts to get up again. "Over there, by the pictures, can you—?" She gestures toward an old-fashioned lamp, the kind with two globes and a chimney, white glass with delicate fading roses painted on it. "You always loved this when you were little—take it with you when you leave today."

I thank her, but ask if she'll save it for me, for the next time I come. It seems bad luck to take it now. And it's funny, I have no memory of admiring its grandmotherly quaintness, its wreath of roses around the lower globe.

Nana has small hands, the fingers thickened by work and age. It's strange to see those hands quiet in her lap, even for a minute, but with the arthritis, she tells me, she can't crochet anymore. I ask about her garden—the little patio at the back of her house where she used to grow lemons, chili peppers, and herbs and bright flowers. By way of answer, she laughs and rolls up her pants legs to show me her knees. There is a long white scar across each of them, where, she says, the doctor put the metal in. "No more gardening for me," she says, "And now the hips aren't so good." Her hands rise a little off her lap; "Oh, *mi hija,*" she says. "Boring, boring! Who wants to hear it? Tell me how you are—how is your little girl?" Her hands flutter; they have so much to tell. Whole histories have passed through them, through her plantings, her cooking, her tenderness with children.

It's Nana's hands I remember best from childhood, their quickness as she helped my mother fold laundry or, on our birthdays, dipped them into little bowls of cheese, onions, and tomatoes to fill hot, crisp tortillas. Her hands moved even faster when she showed me how she once made tortillas in her auntie's Nogales *tortillaria.* She made this into a patty-cake game when I was small, and when I was old enough to hear her stories, she used them to show how, at the age of eight, she carried tall stacks of fresh tortillas on her head, from one end of Nogales to the other. Her arm rose like a dancer's, the hand curved protectively high over an invisible burden.

My daughter is doing well, I tell Nana. She's with her dad this week, for his family's Christmas, but I promise to bring her soon for a visit. I bring out Hannah's first-grade picture, and she holds it for a long time. "So fast," she says. "So fast. Bring her soon."

I will. I want Hannah to hear Nana, to see how someone can shape a story from a life, how a person can tell a story without bitterness or blame—this is a rare thing now, I think.

From Nana I learned that the San Gabriel valley was a wild place once, full of stories. Fugitive lovers and mountain bandits, greedy silver miners, Franciscan padres, railroad kings— suddenly my home felt like a foreign place where anything could happen, and did. Fertile Indian lands became Spanish ranchos, then the pleasure grounds of rich white Victorian businessmen. There were orange and walnut groves, artesian wells and cattle and racehorses; silver and gold in the chapparal-spotted canyons of the San Gabriel Mountains. At the foot of these mountains lay the San Gabriel Mission, with its own strange history of grace and cruelty: the harboring of exhausted explorers and wounded rebels; the punishment of scandalous young ladies, who were shorn of their hair and made to stand in the courtyard for viewing before mass. Nana told me everything she remembered or heard, not waiting for me to grow up. There was the story of the young and charming Doña Maria del Rosario Villa de Felix, wife of a powerful ranchero in the 1830s. *Felix*, said Nana. *It's supposed to mean happiness, but believe me, the name was cursed.* This Maria had the misfortune to fall in love with a young man named Gervasio Alipas. Her husband, Don Domingo, found out about it, and Maria sought sanctuary at the mission. This was long ago, Nana said, and the padres had no choice but to call for her husband, who came by horse to fetch her home. The story ended violently, for Gervasio was hiding in an arroyo near the rancho. He threw his reata over Don Domingo's head, and killed him with his stiletto. Doña Maria helped to bury the body. Children discovered the fugitives in a shadowy oak glade, and so the lovers were caught and executed, their bodies displayed for two hours at the entrance of the city jail. "They say the whole city of Los Angeles turned out to gape at them," Nana used to say. "It's too sad and terrible."

"Do you believe in ghosts, Nana?" I asked her once. "No, not really, *muchacha*," she said. "But I tell you this: I pray every night that the spirits of the dead will have some peace and leave us alone."

Place is forever changed by story. No—by the storyteller. There is no such thing as an ordinary suburb. Our houses, our yards, lie on ancient layers of passion and drama. Beneath my fifth-grade saddle shoes lay the blood of Don Domingo, also the history of his power and rage. And Doña Maria: how crazy she must have looked, begging the padres to hide her; how terribly she must have wanted to be free. Only the storyteller's grace can restore her to us. Hope goes precisely as deep as the teller's generosity: it lives in her amazement and pleasure in the hundred possible versions of one event; in her knowledge that the world cannot be simply or easily known.

Nana was rarely a figure in the stories she told. This fact seems important, part of the gift of her telling. She would begin by saying, "This didn't happen to me, but to my husband's brother. It's true, all of it." She told them to me in our own house, in the well-to-do suburb a mile away from here, the town we'd moved to after I was born. Though I have forgotten or misremembered the stories themselves, I remember exactly her face and body as she told them, the ritual she went through, at each story's beginning. First she would wrap her mother's old black shawl over her head and shoulders and look at me with wide, stricken eyes. Every gesture was theatrical and doubly alive against the formal backdrop of my mother's pale gold draperies, her Japanese panels, the neat cabinets that shut with a click. Just before Nana began a story she would close all the curtains in the living room, to keep the spirits of the dead from eavesdropping, for they were easily upset. This prickled the hairs on my neck: the spirits so real, like volatile neighbors who'd take vengeance if they caught you gossiping about them.

Now when she tells a story, it takes longer. She starts one, then loops into another, leaves it incomplete, adds a bit more to the first, begins a third, goes back to the second. It is a heartbreaking structure, the storytelling of the old. She is a Scheherazade, and looks with fear and longing at the little tape

she got the idea I could work for the doctor's wife and pay
off. It was in the days, you know, when the man still came
ound with a block of ice, and big tongs . . . oh, she wanted
at refrigidaire!"

Refrigidaire—the word is her own. I love it as I love the
bsolute difference of the two versions: the way my father
akes of Nana a legend of patience, and she, in turn, dismisses
rself as a main character, more interested, finally, in the
st era of the iceman with his tongs than her own role as
inderella to her mother's dream of a fridge.

But it was Nana's ghost stories that had the thing I really
raved, the quality missing from my own family's storytelling
ulture. It was the vein of humor, not to mention the pure
leasure of a good scare. There was never a "moral" attached.
Her stories had about them no clear educational urgency;
either were they simply entertainment. They were about the
vay people behaved, and the strange marvel of their actions
n the world. Each story ended in a crescendo of surprise: an
isn't that something?" that hovered like the high note of a vi-
lin, the passionate last burst of a sonata. No denouement, no
ownslope. No ending.

ometime in the mid-eighties, Nana put heavy wrought-iron
grills on the windows and on the front screen door, the one
hat looks out onto Mission Boulevard and the train tracks.
Oh, we have the gangs now," she said. "They roam around,

recorder. Who, on the verge of mortality, would ever willingly
end a story?

This one doesn't really belong to me. . . . I heard it from my hus-
band, who was a boy in this valley long before there was cars or ref-
rigidaires. But listen, Joe told me that when this place was full of
orange groves . . . and Lucky Baldwin owned most of the land here . . .
he was a famous ladies' man, you know, loved women, horses, and any-
thing to do with the Spanish people . . .

So begins the story of the three ladies. It takes place in the
late twenties, on the great ranch, long after Baldwin himself
was dead. Baldwin was a Victorian entrepreneur: he bred racehorses and built the Santa Anita racetrack, among other things.
But he was famous all the way to New York for his escapades
with beautiful young women. "Three Ladies" always starts out
the same way: *This was a long time ago, a dark night, very rainy,*
you know, and hard to see. Joe was just a little boy, in the back of his
uncle's Ford, you know, the old kind, a Model T, with a rumble seat and
everything. Joe and his cousins were in the rumble seat, and this is
what they saw. They were driving over a little bridge on the Baldwin
ranch—when you go there now, I don't know if the bridge is still
there, but anyway, the lights of the little car flashed across something,
and you know what it was they saw on that bridge? Three ladies, all
in black dresses, old-fashioned, you know, from Lucky Baldwin's time,
with the big bustles, and those big black hats with veils, you know, so
you couldn't see the face. As they drove past in the car, the bridge was
so narrow, you know, that the ladies pressed themselves against the

bridge rails, like so, to not be hit. . . . The grown-ups saw it too, from the front seat—it wasn't just the children. Everybody saw it. And then, of course, when they looked back again, there was nobody on the bridge. No ladies. Nobody on the bridge at all.

What I love about this story is the image of the three ladies, their faces hidden by the netting of their great dark hats, by the rain and the late hour itself. A midnight impression of falling rain, a little bridge, a sweeping curve of black crinoline. The moment is held still, a visitation, dreamlike and without action, then vanished. I have asked Nana if she knew that Lucky Baldwin had a series of notorious suits brought against him in the 1880s by three beautiful young women who claimed he'd promised to marry them. She shook her head and smiled dreamily at me as if the scandalous facts were of no concern. "Certainly it's true, *muchacha*, that he loved womens. My God, he loved them, especially the ones with dark hair and small feet."

I want to say that I don't come from a storytelling family, but this is not precisely true. My parents practiced their own particular kind of storytelling: aphoristic, self-deprecating, punctuated by a shrug to deflate any high expectation. My mother's stories were marbled with warnings; chiefly I re-member stories of family tragedies, of suicides and cancers, particularly tragedies afflicting the young. She told these in a tone of quiet amazement, her very manner emphasizing the

secret lesson of all our tribe's stories. You had t[...] the worst; at any minute life could knock you[...] were built of the same materials—tragedies a[...] in his, there was always a miraculous rescue a[...] was even a tale of his own kidnapping as a [...] New Jersey—a story whose details are now lo[...] as my mother says, very little, if any, is true. [...] young, it all seemed utterly true. His voice w[...] offhand, it constituted a form of realism all its[...]

Even the story of how Nana came to us—[...] phrase my family uses, *not* how we came to h[...] different in my parents' combined telling, and [...] version, Mrs. Rodriguez, herself a mother of tv[...] father's office with a sinus infection she'd had [...] father looked in her ear and was shocked by h[...] so terrible was the inflammation. As they talk[...] tantly admitted that she and her husband we[...] their family and her own mother on his mechani[...] times weren't so easy just then. My father said,[...] go down Almansor Street and see my wife—she[...] with the house and the children, and could use y[...] can bring your children along, no problem."

Nana laughed when I told her this version. "T[...] right," she said. "But I don't remember no infectio[...] any pain. It was my own mother who went to him[...] doctor, that's how it happened. She wanted a new[...]